Charles Dickens and Premchand

Novelists with a Social Purpose

Charles Dickens and Premchand

Novelists with a Social Purpose

PRAMILA BATRA

PRESTIGE

PRESTIGE BOOKS
3/28, East Patel Nagar
New Delhi 110 008

ISBN: 81-7551-101-X

Printed at Chaman Offset Press, New Delhi 110 002

CONTENTS

Preface
7

**Charles Dickens and Premchand:
The Social Background**
9

**The Depiction of Social Problems and
Their Solution in the Novels of
Dickens and Premchand**
33

**The Social Purpose of
Dickens and Premchand**
61

**The Technique in the Novels of
Dickens and Premchand**
81

**The Achievement of
Dickens and Premchand**
98

Preface

Art for life's sake is regarded by some as second-rate literature. Even such a great literary figure as George Bernard Shaw is sometimes run down as a propagandist. Dickens and Premchand also wrote novels with a purpose but to put them in the category of propagandists is to belittle their importance as creative artists. In their hands, the novel was only a literary means through which they could draw the attention of masses towards the social problems. Their purpose in writing novels was to elevate humanity at large and to ameliorate the condition of distressed people.

Dickens and Premchand have commanded enormous respect from literary critics who have estimated their genius individually. The present book attempts a comparative and critical appraisal of their art and ideas. It is hoped that it will present the two great authors in a new perspective, benefitting scholars of both English and Hindi literature.

The first chapter introduces the two writers, Charles Dickens and Premchand, and the milieu in which they lived. The next chapter highlights the attitudes of Dickens and Premchand towards the various social, economic and political problems confronting their respective societies. The third chapter deals with the purpose behind their literary careers. The penultimate chapter brings out the contrast in the different techniques adopted by the two writers. The final chapter focusses attention on the ultimate outcome of their literary battle against the problems prevailing in their respective societies.

I cannot close these prefatory remarks without acknowledging my indebtedness to those who helped me in the preparation of this book. I am grateful to Dr. D.S. Sharma, Prof. Chaman Nahal, Dr. R.K. Dhawan, Dr. B.B. Jain, and Dr. Suman Bala for their invaluable help. I thank Prestige Books for bringing out my book so elegantly.

PRAMILA BATRA

Charles Dickens and Premchand: The Social Background

Charles Dickens (1812-1870) was born on 7 February 1812 in Mile End Terrace at Portsea, near Portsmouth, where his father John Dickens was a clerk in the Navy Pay Office. The family moved to London in 1814 and stayed there for three years. In 1817, they shifted to Chatham where John held a responsible post in the government dockyard. They lived here for a period of six years, which was the happiest time in the life of young Charles.

Charles was a sickly child, suffering from spasmodic attacks. His ill health cut him off from the society of other boys and made him more than usually self-centred, which explains his failure to appreciate his mother and the warmth for his father. John Dickens lacked a sense of money, enjoying a life of comparative ease among jovial companions, borrowing sums, which he could not repay, sacrificing his family's future and comfort. He could never master the art of making both ends meet. Charles's mother, Elizabeth Dickens, was also as spendthrift and muddleheaded. Between 1810 and 1822, she had seven children and an eighth was born in 1827.

When Charles was eight, he with his sister Fanny attended a day school run by one Mr. Giles. John Dickens managed to acquire for him a number of books including *Roderick Random, Peregrine Pickle, Humphrey Clinker, Tom Jones, The Vicar of Wakefield, Robinson Crusoe, The Arabian Nights* and *Don Quixote.* This was his chief education at that time and the main solace of his life. In *David Copperfield,* Charles Dickens writes of the influence they made on him: "They kept alive my fancy and my hope of something beyond that place and this."[1]

Charles had pleasant memories of his schooling with William Giles. Giles, who had been at Oxford and was an accomplished scholar, recognised Charles's unusual aptitude and did his best to train the boy's mind.

Early in 1823, the family left for London without Charles who may have been in the middle of a school term, but he followed them later in the year. John Dickens had been recalled for duty at Somerset House and was probably glad to leave his Chatham creditors. But Charles was deeply grieved by the move. Having to leave school at the age of eleven was a dreadful blow to him. Charles had to clean the family boots, look after his younger brothers and sisters, do household work and run errands. He felt completely isolated and absolutely neglected.

Spendthrift ways of John Dickens caught up with him. His easy temper, gregarious disposition and tendency to lavish hospitality on all and sundry produced want and misery for the family. Charles never forgave the behaviour of his mother, who deserved nothing but praise for her hopeless struggle to keep things going when everything had gone wrong.

Mrs. Dickens did her best when the crisis came but her best amounted to nothing. She decided to open a school. She rented a house in Gower Street North and placed a brass plate with the words "Mrs. Dickens' Establishment." But the efforts of Mrs. Dickens to increase the family income failed and the family sometimes faced near starvation. Meanwhile, there was trouble with the butcher and the baker who had the curious notion that their bills ought to be paid. Charles could never forget this time. He wrote once to Forster:

> I know, I don't exaggerate unconsciously and unintentionally the scantiness of my resources and the difficulties of my life. . . . I know that if a shilling or so is given to me by anyone, I spend it in a dinner or a tea.[2]

The things went so badly that the home in Gower Street was gradually emptied of its furniture. Charles was compelled to pay many visits to the pawnshops. The first thing to go were his books, which were followed by chairs, pictures, crockery and so on, until the family had to camp in two uncarpeted rooms. And ultimately, the poor boy, now eleven years old, had to go out to earn his living at Warren's Blacking Factory, London, at the salary of six shillings a week.

It was a shattering blow to be castaway at such an age, with all early hopes of learning and distinction crushed. His work was simple, it consisted of tying up bottles neatly and sticking labels on them. Dickens wrote to Forster:

> My work was to cover the pots of paste blacking, first with a piece of oil paper, and then with a piece of blue paper, to tie them with a string and then to clip the paper close and neat, all round until it looked as smart as a pot of ointment from an apothecary's shop.

In his autobiographical novel, *David Copperfield*, Dickens recalls:

> It was a crazy old house with a warf of its own abutting on the water when the tide was in and on the mud when the tide was out and literally overrun with rats. Its panelled rooms discoloured with the dirt of 100 years, I dare say its decaying floors and staircase; the squeaking and scuffling of the old grey rats down in the cellars and the dirt and

> rottenness of the place are things not of many years ago in my mind but of present instant. (154)

Dickens worked hard there from eight in the morning till eight in the night. A fortnight after Charles had become a wage drudge, the long expected blow fell and John Dickens at the suit of James Karr was arrested at Marshalsea prison for £ 10. Charles ran backwards and forwards between his father and his distracted family, his eyes streaming with tears, trying to control his sobs. Later on, when his father realised that the sensitive heart of his son was on the point of breaking, arrangements were made for his lodging near the prison.

When John's mother died, £ 500 of the invested saving went to William, brother of John. He at once paid £ 40 to the Court for James Karr and thus effected his brother's discharge. After his release from jail, John Dickens at once applied to his brother-in-law J.H. Barrow, editor of the *Mirror of Parliament*, for work as a political reporter and was fortunately appointed a reporter of the British paper. This enabled him to continue paying fee at a school to which he had admitted Charles. He resumed his study at Wellington House Academy at Hempstead Board. Here he passed some of the happy days of his life.

At the age of fifteen, Charles left school and joined a firm of solicitors as an office apprentice but very soon he realised that this job could not fulfil his ambitions. In eighteen months, he left the solicitor's office and became a professional shorthand writer. To begin with, he got a job in the court of law where he acquired much of his knowledge of the intricacies of law as well as his contempt for it.

But shorthand was not his only interest. For a time Charles, partly from love of the stage and partly with the idea of becoming a professional actor, spent all his spare evenings at the theatre. Soon, because of his great speed and accuracy in shorthand, he became a reporter in the press gallery of the House of Commons. From the press gallery, he looked down on the final parliamentary skirmishes over the Reform Bill of 1832, and in doing so earned twenty-five guineas a week. He developed as low an opinion of parliament as he had previously formed of courts of law.

After working for a year in the gallery, Charles began to set things down as they struck him in a very homely and even ordinary way. His work showed a relish for the common stuff of human nature. He called these jottings sketches; they were to begin with snapshots of actual people and actual occurrences and then were given their leading characteristic. He had also been appointed to the regular staff of a newspaper (*The Morning Chronicle*.) He reported parliamentary proceedings. He travelled up and down the country, covering elections, great political meetings and other events. His first book *Sketches by Boz* appeared in 1836. It revealed him as a close observer of the human scene, gifted with an expansive form of humour that was to make him famous.

In April, Dickens married Catherine. Quiet, silent and unenterprising, Catherine had dull friends and as she never developed the social gift of discriminating between one person and another, she was incapable later on of playing her part as the celebrity's wife. Their marriage proved a failure. Dickens wrote to his friend John Forster: "Poor Catherine and I are not made for each other and there is no help for it." (II, 198)

His next work, which appeared in monthly instalments, was *Pickwick Papers*. This book made Dickens instantaneously famous. As John Foster comments: "Let me add that there was something more in it all than the gratification of mere fun and laughter, or even then the rarer pleasure that underlies the outbreak of all forms of genuine humour . . . and it took not many more to make clear to the intelligent reader that a new and original genius in the walk of Smollett and Fielding had arisen in England." (I, 73)

The anniversary of the birth of *Pickwick Papers* was preceded by a personal grief, which profoundly moved Charles. His wife's next younger sister, Mary, who lived with them and by sweetness of nature had made herself the ideal of his life, died with a terrible suddenness that for the time completely bore him down.[3] In all the descriptions of deaths in his novels, we get reminders of his sufferings.

During the autumn of 1837, Dickens worked hard at *Oliver Twist*, edited the Memoirs of Grimaldi, and dedicated it to his father. Further, the journey to Yorkshire was made to gather material for *Nicholas Nickleby*. There he studied the whole system and conditions of Yorkshire schools and schoolmasters.

At the invitation of Washington Irving, Dickens left for the U.S.A., where people accorded him an enthusiastic reception. His financial difficulties forced him to sell the fourth share in his work for the next eight years to Messers Bradbury and Evans for £ 2800. In 1846, he went to Paris, where he met elder Dumas, Victor Hugo and others. He began *David Copperfield* in 1846 and became the editor of a newly started magazine *Household Words*.

Dickens's novels can be divided into three groups: those written before his visit to the United States in 1842, those written after his return, and before his separation. In the first group are *Sketches by Boz*, *The Pickwick Papers*, *Oliver Twist*, *Nicholas Nickleby*, *The Old Curiosity Shop* and *Barnaby Rudge*; the books with which he conquered the world in the second group are: *Martin Chuzzlewit*, *Dombey and Son*, *The Five Christmas Books*, *David Copperfield*, *Bleak House*, *Hard Times* and *Little Dorrit*; in the third group: *A Tale of Two Cities*, *Great Expectations*, *Our Mutual Friend* and *Edwin Drood*.

One Sunday morning, he attended the meeting of delegates in the cockpit and on Monday he went to see the strike pay distributed and then to an open-air meeting. Walter Landor had sailed for the Indies. His father was reading a Christmas Carol to an enraptured audience at Manchester and deriving immense pleasure therefrom. He was receiving overtures too from Manchester magnets begging him to produce a play again in their city. Most willingly did he agree to do so and applied to Wigan, the manager of the Olympic theatre for a substitute and on his recommendation, engaged Mrs. Ternan and her two daughters Maria and Ellen for the parts. Ellen appeared to him most attractive and a sweet little thing. She, with her sympathetic blue eyes, took up such a worshipping attitude and seemed so pathetically anxious to interpret every line according to Dickens's' wishes that she completely captivated him.

After a few rehearsals, Dickens's emotional equilibrium was upset. In *Uncle John*, he had to load his bride with wonderful presents and his impersonator found it irresistible to give his sweet little friend some real jewellery. Kate Dickens, who knew the plot, realised what must have been going on when a bracelet ordered for Ellen was delivered to her by mistake. It annoyed her extremely. When she flared up, Charles told her to believe in the innocence of the girl. Katey, the second girl, tells us that when she passed by her parents's bedroom, she heard sobs of her mother and when she asked why she was crying, she replied "Your father has asked me to go and see Ellen Ternan." "You shall not go," said Katey stamping her foot but Mrs. Dickens did as she was asked.[4]

At the time of separation, Kate was forty-three years old and Charles was forty-six. At this time, Georgy, sister-in-law of Dickens, proved immensely useful to Dickens. She kept his house together. She had Mamey and Katey (Dickens's daughters) under her thumb and managed to please them by her cheerfulness.

On finishing *Our Mutual Friend* in 1865, Dickens light-heartedly polished off a Christmas story "Dr. Marigold's Prescriptions" and then devoted his attention exclusively to preparing new readings. On St. Valentine's day, 1866, Dickens took the chair at annual dinner of the dramatic Equestrian and Musical Fund of Willis rooms. He spoke of the professional brotherhood that honoured the claims of kindred in the dingiest and dirtiest concert room in the least lucid theatre in the raggedest circus tent ever stained by weather.

Soon after this, Dickens felt himself to be unwell. The doctor said that he was suffering from irritability of heart but the observable symptoms were great pain and lameness of one leg. Even in such condition of ill health, he went on a tour of the British Isles and Paris. A year after his return from America saw the commencement of the work, which was finally interrupted by his death. He worked on *Edwin Drood*, all the day of his seizure, sitting up at his desk in the chalet. That night at dinner Georgy, his only companion, realised that he was looking desperately ill. A few minutes later, he had a stroke from which he never regained consciousness. His daughters Mamey and Katey were summoned from London and the next day Katey was sent back to break the news to her mother. She returned in company with Ellen Ternan. In a moving account of his sad demise, Forster wrote:

> The terrible news from England, wrote Longfellow to me (Cambridge Mass 12 June 1870), filled us all with inexpressible sadness. Dickens was so full of life that it did not seem possible he could die and yet he has gone before us, and we are sorrowing for him. . . . I never knew an author's death cause such general mourning. . . . I borrow the

> expression from the bishop of Manchester, who on the third day after Dickens's death in the Abbey where he was so soon to be laid, closed a plea for the toleration of differences of opinion where the foundations of religious truth are accepted with these words: "If in the simplest and briefest words I allude to that said and unexpected death which has robbed English literature of one of its highest living ornaments!" (II, 314-15)

This brief account of Dickens's life reflects the various events which deeply affected and shaped Dickens's literary career. Let us now turn to some important events in the life of Premchand.

In the hamlet of Lamhi, four miles from Banaras, Premchand (1880-1936) was born in a middle class Shrivastava (Kayastha) family. Father Ajaiblal used to call him by the name of Dhanpat Rai and uncle as Navab Rai. His mother Anandi Devi gave birth to three daughters. Two of them died in infancy and the third one survived the parents.

The boy was born after three sisters, and it was a belief that such a child proves unlucky for one of his parents. What an irony of fate, that the boy who had to fight throughout his life against the dead conventions of society, himself was born, under the shadow of a silly superstition!

In the loving care of his mother and grandmother, the days did pass smoothly, but in the very first attack of asthma, his mother fell ill and left this world after about six months. Ajaiblal was a village postmaster on a salary of ten rupees per month. He was a thoughtful, straightforward and foresighted person but in his last days he blundered badly into marriage. And due to this, Premchand could not free himself from the shackles of poverty throughout his life.

Premchand's life was not a bed of roses and his early acquaintance with suffering prepared him to face the gross realities of life, which later on became the mainspring of inspiration for his creative art.

His primary education was accomplished in Lamhi. Small schools were there, where Munshis used to teach Urdu and Persian. Hindi was also taught up to fifth class. Premchand studied Urdu in the village and after that, he came to Gorakhpur, because of the transfer of his father. He reminisces:

> I must have been in my early teens. I didn't know Hindi at all. I had a passion for Urdu novels. Maulana Sharar, Ratan Nath Sarshar, Mirza Rusva and Maulavi Mohammed Ali were the most popular novelists of that time. Wherever I used to get their writings, I forgot all about my schools. The only job was to finish the book.[5]

In his early teens, Premchand was an avid reader of the writings of the famous writers of that time. An interesting thing regarding the school was that the Maulavi kept no attendance register. Consequently, if some student played truant, there was no record, nor any fine for truancy. Premchand and his cousin, who was older to him by two years, were no exceptions.

The pathetic story of the child, who lost his mother at such a tender age, can be written only in tears. In spite of poverty and lack of parental love, Premchand struggled on to achieve the goal of his life, which was to become an author. Moreover, his heart always wailed for his mother. Such atmosphere embittered his life but he never lost his mental balance. His wife Shiv Rani Devi writes: "Sometimes I used to get angry. All family members created problems for him. But he did not care. He bore it all very patiently and with a smiling face."

Premchand's inexhaustible fund of patience sometimes irritated his wife Shiv Rani. After staying in Gorakhpur for sometime, Premchand came to Banaras due to the transfer of his father and was admitted in Queen's College in the ninth class. At that time, he was about fifteen years old. His monthly allowance was five rupees towards the school fees, milk, books, clothes etc. But he dared not ask for more. His stepmother was a terror to him. Money was sorely needed and somehow he sought some tuition work. Rajeshwar Guru writes about Premchand's hard life during his college days when, besides his own study, he had to teach also and walk a long distance on foot in cold winter:

> I got free from school at 3.30 p.m. I was in Kashi's Queen's College. The Headmaster had given full fee concession. Examination was approaching near and I had to take tuition. It was tough winter; I used to reach at 4 o'clock. After taking tuition, I used to get free at 6.00 p.m. Then, at 8 o'clock, after brisk walking, I could reach home which was five miles away in a village. Again, early in the morning at 8 o'clock, I had to start.
>
> I never reached school on time. After taking supper at night, I studied in the light of an earthen lamp and feeling exhausted fell asleep. (28)

Apart from this, by arranging the marriage of his son, Ajaiblal created responsibilities for his young son, which the latter was not strong to shoulder. Premchand's wife was the daughter of a Zamindar. When the couple travelled back home by a camel-driven cart, Premchand was shocked to find that his wife was dark and ugly—her face was scarred with small pox. One of her shoulders was higher than the other. She limped and was older in age.

After six months, Ajaiblal was transferred to Lucknow. He left his family at Lamhi, but to add to his woes, Ajaiblal, a chronic patient, returned to Lamhi for treatment. His six months's illness cost the family its entire savings. And when

Ajaiblal died at the age of 56, it was with great financial difficulty that his last rites were performed.

With the family coffers empty, it was Premchand's lot to support not only his wife but also the stepmother and her two sons. He was also to pursue his studies. The only way open to him was to coach the junior students privately. The headmaster obliged him by giving a freeship. Under such tough circumstances, he could pass his matriculation examination in the second division. He was no longer entitled to a freeship at college. Consequently, admission to the Queen's College, Banaras, was out of question.

Premchand shifted to a small room in Banaras, bought a kerosene oil lamp and the only furniture he had was a gunny bag. Premchand would cook khichri once a day, eat it and then cleanse the utensils. On one occasion, when he had no money for two days, he took out his help book for Chakravarti's book on Arithmetic, went to a bookseller and sold it at half the price. By chance, a moustached gentleman, the headmaster of a mission school at Chunargarh, offered to Premchand the job of an assistant teacher at Rs. 18/- a month. The job was much above Premchand's expectations and he accepted it immediately.

Premchand joined but did not continue for long at the school at Chunargarh. He got a job in the district school at Bahraich to teach the students of fifth class. His salary was fixed at twenty rupees a month. Later, Premchand was transferred to Pratap Garh where he served for the next twenty-two months. There, he succeeded in making arrangement for undergoing teacher's training.

In 1904 he passed Junior English Teacher's examination in first division. He also passed the special vernacular examination in Urdu as well as in Hindi from the Allahabad University.

Nine months after his return to Pratap Garh, Premchand was called back to teach at the Model School, attached to the Central

Training College at Allahabad. After three months, in May 1905, he was sent on promotion to teach the students of eighth class at the district school at Kanpur.

Premchand had started writing in Urdu and his articles started appearing in the magazine *Zamana* whose editor Munshi Daya Narayan Nigam encouraged him a lot. Premchand began to live in a house in his neighbourhood. There used to be regular literary gatherings in the office of *Zamana* and he never missed these. Nigam recalls the time spent in the office of *Zamana* as the best period in Premchand's life. It was the place where various friends and companions used to assemble in the evening for two to three hours and no aspect of current world affairs was left untouched.[7]

By this time, Premchand had become the father of a daughter. His financial condition was not so difficult. In 1910, he became a helping teacher in a Government school and, around 1918, he was appointed on the post of Sub Deputy Inspector of Schools.

Robbed early of parental love and care, steeped in poverty, crushed under the heavy responsibilities of family and the tyrannies of his stepmother who contributed to make his married life miserable, the young mind of Premchand responded to those forces which sought to bring about radical changes in the social, economic and religious fabric of India. His first novel *Asrari Mabbid* was published under the name of Dhanpat Rai. Other novels were *Pratap Chandra*, *Prema* and *Krishna*.

Nigam tells us that Premchand wrote *Zamana*'s popular monthly column entitled "Raftar-e-Zamana" on current affairs in national and international world. His early short stories are "Roothi Rani," "Yehi Mera Vatan Hai," "Sheikhi Makhmoor," "Silai Maatam" and "Isha-e-Dunia Aur Hubbevatan."

Premchand's domestic life was not happy. There were bickerings and ugly scenes between his stepmother and his wife.

The chief reason was the tyranny of his stepmother over his unfortunate wife with whom he had pulled on uncomplainingly as all traditional husbands do. His wife was adamant that she would no longer live in the same house and she must go to her parents. Premchand made arrangement for her departure. Since then there was no communication between them.

Within three or four days of his wife's departure, the parents of Premchand's stepmother insisted that he should marry again. But he had determined this time to marry a widow. And just by chance one day he came across an advertisement in the matrimonial columns from Munshi Devi Prasad of Salempur village regarding his daughter who had been married at the age of eleven and widowed three months after marriage. Premchand sent particulars about his education and salary and offered to accept the child widow in wedlock.

His first book published by Zamana press was *Soze Vatan*. The imprint line of the publisher and the printer was left out inadvertently. The offence was a serious one and the Criminal Investigation Department of State set about the task of probing into the matter. The Collector asked Premchand to give him a gist of each story; and on learning about the contents, he was furious. Premchand was ordered to hand over all the copies of the book to the government and also never to think of writing anything without the government's prior permission.

The restrictions imposed on Navab Rai were irksome. Nevertheless, as a government servant, he had to abide by the rules. So he began to write under the name of Premchand. He was careful that everything written under this name was published in *Zamana* only. The first story written by Premchand was "Bade Ghar Ki Beti." Later, he wrote "Ah-e-Bekas," "Mamta," "Alime Be Amal" and "Manzil Maqsood."

It is necessary here to refer briefly to Premchand's effort to secure higher education. He aspired to take a master's degree.

Being a teacher, he could appear as a private candidate and he luckily got through the B.A. examination in the second division in 1916. Premchand was transferred on promotion in August 1916 to become the Assistant Teacher at the High school, Gorakhpur. He became quite popular with his colleagues as well as his students.

In 1920-21, Non-cooperation movement was at its zenith. The blood of freedom was surging in the veins of Indians. Meetings were held at several places. This movement was inspired by Mahatma Gandhi who wanted freedom through non-violence. Premchand was deeply influenced by Mahatma Gandhi and he resigned his government job. The headmaster of the school constantly insisted that Premchand should withdraw his resignation but Premchand remained undaunted. The headmaster asked him to consult his wife. "She has been consulted," said Premchand and in fact she had encouraged him to resign. Shiv Rani Devi writes: "This is not a one-sided affair, the whole country is involved in it, despite that, there is sacrifice and dedication in it, one can do it voluntarily." (50)

Shiv Rani always remained a source of strength and inspiration to Premchand. She encouraged him to pursue his course independently and not to be deterred by the encumbrance of unemployment. Premchand joined as headmaster in a Maharashtrian school but left this and began to live in Lamhi. After sometime, he came to Kashi and became headmaster in Kashi Vidyapeeth at a monthly salary of Rs. 135. It was during this period that he wrote his novels *Sevasadan* (1918), *Premashram* (1922), *Rangbhumi* (1924).

After reaching Lucknow in 1924, he edited *Madhuri* and completed *Gaban* and *Kayakalp*. Later, he established his press and edited *Jagaran* in 1932 on Diwali. *Hans* was also published from there. Later, he printed *Karambhumi* (1932) and his last novel *Godan* (1936). But unfortunately, the press suffered losses and Premchand decided to either close it or sell it off. Due to ill health, he handed over *Hans* to Bharatiya Sahitya Parishad. In his lifetime only, Parishad also stopped its publication when the government asked for the bail. This came as a severe shock to him and he began to remain sick. While ailing seriously, Premchand worried over the future of *Hans*. He asked Shiv Rani to continue its publication. Shiv Rani records the following conversation in her book:

Premchand: You arrange for the bail of *Hans*. After getting well, I will look after it.

Shiv Rani: First you recover, everything will be all right then.

Premchand: No, arrange for the bail. I may survive or not. *Hans* has to be there. This will be my monument. (228)

But there was no money and *Hans* could not continue.

With the publication of *Hans* and several short stories, Premchand became highly renowned. Great authors recognised him and in the field of novel, he became famous as "King of Novels." He was invited to accept the Chairmanship of different societies. In May 1934, when he was in Kashi, a film company invited him. This was the only way of income now.

Premchand went to Bombay but found it very difficult to write stories for films. He found that even when a story was good, it could not be made into a good film unless suitable actors were available. The film *Mill Majdoor* was released but remained unsuccessful. Another story he wrote was for the film *Navjeevan* but this film also failed at the box office.

The health of Premchand was deteriorating and his wife did not agree to his undertaking a trip overseas. He stayed there for one year because he had incurred debts and hoped to clear them. In 1935, he was invited by Hindi Prachar Sabha of Madras and then to Kashi. With the cooperation of Satya Jeevan Verma, he started a literary society called "Lekhak Sangh" (Writers's Forum) and was elected its first president.

In May 1936, *Godan* was completed. Later, Premchand started a novel *Mangal Sutra.* In August 1936, he was to deliver a speech at a meeting organised on the occasion of Gorky's death. Since he was not keeping well, his wife asked him to take rest. Premchand told his wife: "Shiv Rani, you are mistaken. What can an author divide and distribute? The writer has only perseverance, which he can pass on to others. All are benefitted by this dedication of the author and it results in the welfare of people." (252)

Premchand always thought that all that a writer can do is to dedicate himself to his creative work. He had great regard for Gorky and delivered his last speech on 25th June 1936. One day, Premchand vomitted blood and since then his sleep fled away. As he had lost all hopes of survival, Premchand asked Shiv Rani to bring pen and paper. When she inquired, Premchand spoke in a broken voice:

> "Let me arrange for your maintenance!"
>
> I said: "Don't think so much, relax, you will be alright!"
>
> He said: "No, bring these," and he broke down. Tears flowed down my eyes too. When I laid him down on a cot, he fell unconscious and could not open his eyes again.

On October 8,1936, the earthly career of the great and glorious Hindi writer came to an end. His last novel, *Godan*, through the life story of Hori, depicts the sad saga of his own pathetic life.

The lives of both Premchand and Dickens were smeared with unhappy and pathetic events from which emanated their stori s and novels, which appeal to every human heart.

I n order to obtain a comprehensive view of the stature of Dick ns and Premchand, let us go into the various influences that contributed to the shaping of the literary genius of these novelists.

"A history of English literature," says Compton Rickett, "needs to be based on a background of its social activities in order to be clearly seen and nicely appraised."[8] He observes that the closer approximation of literature to social life is very marked in the Victorian era.

It was in 1776, the year in which the American colonies revolted, that Adam Smith who had won great renown as professor of moral philosophy at Glasgow University, brought out *The Wealth of Nations*. This eighteenth century testament of free enterprise had a profound influence on the British Commonwealth and the United States. It gave the rising commercial and industrial classes an awareness of their own virtues. Adam Smith presented the independent self-reliant merchant or manufacturer as a "National Hero". In pursuing his self-interest, he advanced the general interest. The political parts of *Little Dorrit*, in a sense, are a brilliant dramatisation of Adam Smith.

No member of the society of individualists ever put the case against officialdom with such energy as Meagles, when he came roaring out of the circumlocution office. Dickens's anger against the circumlocution office was the anger of new liberalism against old conservatists. The circumlocution office seemed to represent privilege at its most insolent and indefensible. The ideas of moral philosopher of the middle class Adam Smith, proved irresistible, because the middle class was irresistibly marching to power. And to do them and Adam Smith justice, they believed that they were advancing the cause of humanity and ensuring a happy life for all classes.

The fright caused in Britain in 1792 by the terror in France had brought about a persecution of liberal minds as well as cranks and avowed revolutionaries. But even Pitt and John Scott, the Attorney General, were unable to quench the general enthusiasm of those who had caught fire from the declaration of rights of man. How could the passion of such a celestial flame be easily extinguished?

In the eighteen months after Waterloo riots, civil disturbance broke out in twenty cities and a dozen shires. The Corn Law of 1815 made bread dear at a time when wages were falling and there was much misery and want in both the industrial and rural areas. In the year that Dickens was born, the newspapers reported machines wrecking havoc in the midlands and the north and the meeting of alarmed magistrates to put down the frenzy.

Laissez-Faire had served as a term of contempt and abuse but it is just to recall that it was once again a cry of freedom. The mercantile policy of old conservatism, the restrictive practises imposed by the Navigation-Acts and the Corn Law of 1815 convinced the liberal minded in those days that government interference with trade and commerce represented the negation of liberty.

Apart from this, several reform bills were enacted starting with the year 1832, which progressively granted voting right to more and more people, ultimately ending in universal adult suffrage. As a result, the House of Commons no longer remained an oligarchy. The Victorian age was, so to say, a middle age, which witnessed a gradual change from aristocracy to democracy.

Despite these, there were certain social evils of the time like economic depression, industrialism, unemployment, child labour, the gulf between the rich and the poor. Dickens raised his voice against these. Many of his novels are built around a particular social theme. For instance, *Bleak House* attacks the law delays; *Nicholas Nickleby* the abuses of charity schools and the sadism of schoolmasters; *Hard Times* the pet concepts of the then current political economy; *Little Dorrit* the inhumanities to which poor debtors are often subjected. But above all such social criticism in contemporary context is the basic lesson of humaneness and charity, which almost all Dickens's novels teach implicitly.

Despite many evils like the hardness of heart and the selfishness of those in high places, the greed and hypocrisy, the world for Dickens was still good enough to live in. Nowhere does he say that all is right with the world; but nowhere does he say that all is wrong with the world. He is a realist as well as an optimist.

On the other hand, Premchand was deeply moved by the events following Jallianwala Bagh massacre. When Gandhi visited Gorakhpur, during non-cooperation movement, Premchand along with his wife and children, went to listen to him. A glimpse of Gandhi wrought such a miracle that he got a new incentive and new direction and became a follower of Gandhi. Within a day or two, he responded to the call of Mahatma, asking the teachers and students to leave schools and colleges, the lawyers to leave the courts and the government servants to leave jobs. Premchand decided to resign his job.

Communal harmony was one of the important factors in Gandhi's teaching. Premchand also upheld it and disseminated it through the pages of his novels. He knew that communal disharmony was responsible for the success of the British policy of divide and rule in India. India's freedom remained a far cry till Hindus and Muslims were brought together to forge a common front against the foreign ruler. But unfortunately, the Hindus and the Muslims were shedding each other's blood. Premchand expected wisdom from Hindus because they were in majority. However, the behaviour of Muslims was a stumbling block in the way of communal harmony. And this is exactly what Premchand intended to communicate to his readers.

Under the influence of Gandhi, Premchand undertook to write the story of Surdas, who symbolised the aspirations of the sons of soils by resisting the encroachment of industrialism upon the pious land owned by the great grandfathers. He inculcated Gandhi's philosophy of non-violence and illustrated it in his novels. Through the talk between the hero of *Rangbhumi* and the child Mithua, the history of India unfolds itself. When the hut of Surdas is set ablaze, the following conversation takes place:

> Mithua: And if someone again sets it to fire?
> Surdas: Then we will construct it again.
> Mithua: And if someone does it a thousand times!
> Surdas: We will construct it a thousand times.[9]

This illustrates his stern faith in the Gandhian principles, which advocated non-violent means. In the personality of Surdas, Premchand expresses a great individual. As Vinay, another character in the novel, says: "This is not your hut but our racial temple and we cannot be idle spectators of the devastation of our dear earth."

Apart from Gandhism, Arya Samaj movement also influenced Premchand. Swami Dayanand, the founder of Arya Samaj, propagated the true spirit of Hindu religion based on the Vedas. He sought to banish the silly superstitions and corroding customs from the domain of religion. Moreover, he inspired his countrymen to shatter the fetters of foreign domination and discard the western civilization, which was deforming and disfiguring our culture. He gave a new hope and courage to the people whose spirit had been deadened by centuries of slavery.

The mind of Premchand was moulded by the teachings of Arya Samaj. He exposed the evils of child marriage, dowry, prostitution and the maltreatment meted out to the widows. Arya Samaj believed in the remarriage of young widows. After the demise of his first wife, Premchand married a widow. Through his novels, he tried to eradicate various social evils, which had crept into Hindu society.

Though, chronologically, Dickens was senior to Premchand and he wrote novels in a different milieu, yet we find a deep emotional affinity between them. Good literature transcends the bounds of time and place. Moreover, the circumstances in the nineteenth century England were more or less similar to what India experienced in the early decades of the twentieth century. Both Charles Dickens and Premchand dealt with these social problems afflicting the society of their times.

The Victorian era was an age of rapid flux and baffling complexities. In the words of A.C. Ward: "It was an age of faith and an age of doubt, an age of morality and of hypocrisy, of prosperity and poverty, of idealism and materialism, of progress and decline, of splendour and squalor."[10]

There were two popular agitations in the times of Charles Dickens. The first was the movement, which culminated in the Reform Act of 1832. The second was the movement, which brought the repeal of corn laws in 1846.

In the early nineteenth century, after the Napoleon War, the rural poor in England faced the danger of sheer starvation owing to high prices and low wages. With the introduction of the New Poor Law of 1834, workhouse test was imposed on applicants for public alms. The need to make life in a workhouse less attractive than employment in a factory was the principle on which Commissioners worked and as they could not make employment attractive by enforcing minimum wages, they felt obliged to lower the standard of happiness of the workhouse.

The period of 1834-39 was the administration of the poor law by local boards. The parish officials were converted into social overseers. The new innovations were expected to achieve two beneficial results: to prevent the pauper from breeding in idleness and to compel the able-bodied pauper to work and look for work, thus increasing the supply of labour. The most notorious economy measure of the new poor law was the sparse diet given to the paupers. This makes quite evident the wide gulf between the big capitalists and lower middle-class.

In those days, the bureaucracy and aristocracy often seemed indistinguishable. Moreover, the Industrial Revolution ushered in an era of unprecedented prosperity. But it converted the merry England into a sooty and squalid England.

In fact, Dickens in his novels reflected the marked shift in public opinion and taste. Unemployment and child labour were two severe curses of that era. Lower middle class had no opportunities for earning their livelihood without going through inhuman conditions. It was a period of brutish crimes and savage punishment. There were thieves's dens and the schools for pickpockets. All these conditions are delineated in the novels of Dickens.

And when we turn to the age of Premchand, we find a close proximity between the ages of the two writers. The age of Premchand was a critical period when the fire of freedom had spread furiously among Indians. It was the age of self-awakening and self-recognition. The non-cooperation movement of Mahatma Gandhi had reached its zenith. In the rural areas, the government had placed a new class of landlords between itself and peasants to receive taxes for a certain period. The result was that landlord became the real lord and severe atrocities were inflicted upon the peasants.

Apart from this, there was the corrupt police force. Socially also, India grinded under old orthodoxies and conventions. The condition of women was quite miserable. Dowry, child marriage and the maltreatment of widows were such curses against which Premchand could not resist divulging his sentiments through his writings.

Thus, we see that both Premchand and Dickens were in the mainstream of the contemporary social movements which began and flourished in their times. If Dickens drew a lot from socialism and democracy, Premchand learnt his first political lesson from Gandhism. Dickens became a champion of the downtrodden humanity of the labourers and slumdwellers. Premchand fought for the cause of the poor Indian peasantry, which has been exploited for ages by big landlords. They also exposed the social evils of their time by painting their monstrous faces. To a great extent, their novels gave a rude shock to old values, old ways of thinking and opened a new vista for the coming generations.

NOTES

1. Charles Dickens, *David Copperfield* (New York, 1957), p. 55.
2. John Forster, *The Life of Charles Dickens* (4th ed., New York, 1966), I, p. 25.
3. Her epitaph written by him remains upon a gravestone in the cemetery at Kensal Green: "Young beautiful and good, God numbered her among his angels at the early age of seventeen."
4. G. Story, *Dickens and Daughter*, p. 96.
5. See Rajeshwar Guru, *Premchand Ek Adhyay* (Bhopal, 1958), p. 26.
6. Shiv Rani Devi, *Premchand Ghar Maen* (Delhi, 1956), p. 25.
7. Munshi Daya Narayan Nigam, *Premchand's edition of Zamana* (Kanpur).
8. Compton Rickett, *History of English Literature* (London, 1956), p. 1.
9. Premchand, *Rangbhumi* (Allahabad, 1965), p. 131.
10. A.C. Ward, *Illustrated History of English Literature* (London, 1960), p. 632.

The Depiction of Social Problems and Their Solutions in the Novels of Charles Dickens and Premchand

Both Dickens and Premchand were the true representatives of the respective ages and had a definite social purpose in writing their novels. Their literary works reveal that they were not merely great intuitive observers but penetrating commentators on life. Dickens was a social novelist as well as a social reformer, a pioneer writer of lower-middle-class society and of the life of the town folk in their varied ways. His opinions and ideals were in complete accord with the middle-class opinions of his day.

Edgar Johnson views him as a social critic and the spokesman of masses. He remarks: "The unifying thread of Dickens's entire career was a critical analysis of society and its problem hardly surpassed in grasp or scope either by his contemporaries or by any more recent novelists."[1]

All his novels depict social, political and economic problems: the miseries and children, pitiable conditions of prisons slavery, delay in justice, defective parliamentary system, the gap between the haves and the have nots and the evils of industrialisation. Similar problems existed in India too. These were: dowry, maladjustment in marriage, helplessness of widows, prostitution, untouchability, bribery, moneylenders, corrupt police force, impact of western education and materialism, breaking up of joint family system. Premchand exposed these problems in his novels and short stories.

The Miseries of Childhood

In the early nineteenth century, England experienced rapid industrial growth, which brought in its wake the abuse of child labour. Children were condemned to work in factories and mines for a meagre sum of six shillings a week in very unhealthy conditions. Since labour in outlying places was not so easy to obtain, the owners of workhouses employed poor children as apprentices at low wages. Dickens launched a bitter attack on such inhuman treatment of the children with a somewhat subjective tinge of pain and anguish. George Orwell comments: "No one, at any rate, no English writer has written better about childhood than Dickens. In spite of the fact that the children are now comparatively sanely treated, no novelist has shown the same power of entering into the child's point of view."[2]

In *David Copperfield*, he has given a piquant and pathetic description of the children's exploitation and working of Murdstone and Grinby's Warehouse. *Oliver Twist* is a classic novel about the abuse of child labour and the cruelty of the masters of the workhouse. When Oliver was nine, he was taken back to workhouse. Diet in workhouse, especially given to children, was completely inadequate. After a draw of lots, it was decided to entrust Oliver with the duty of asking the master of the workhouse for more gruel. Oliver did so and caused great commotion:

> There was a general start. Horror was depicted on every countenance.
>
> "For more," said Mr. Limokins, "compose yourself Bumble and answer me distinctly. Do I understand that he asked for more after he had eaten the supper allotted by the dietary."
>
> "He did, Sir," replied Bumble.

> "That boy will be hung," said the gentleman in the white waistcoat. "I know that boy will be hung."[3]

Nicholas Nickleby is about the suffering children in the oppressive educational institutions. Dickens has presented very realistically the picture of Yorkshire schools where children were supposed to be improved and reformed. Mr. Squeers, a cruel schoolmaster, is not an individual but represents a class. Every student of his class is terrified.

> In a corner of the seat was a very small trunk tied round with a scanty piece of cord and on the trunk was perched his lace up half boots and corduroy trousers dangling in the air, a diminutive boy with his shoulders drawn upto his ears and his hands planted on his knees who glanced timidly at the schoolmasters from time to time, with evident dread and apprehension.[4]

Apart from the deplorable conditions in workhouses and factories, every kind of education existing in England gets a mauling at Dickens's hands. Flogging was a common method of punishing a child. The picture of Mr. Creakle's school in *David Copperfield* gives us a vivid picture of the school life and the working of a child's mind.

> School began in earnest the next day. Mr. Creakle came to where I sat and told me that I was famous for biting too. He then showered me the cane and asked me what I thought of that for a tooth. Was it sharp, hey? Did it bite, hey? At every question he gave me a cut with it that made me writhe. So I was very soon introduced to Salem House (as Steerforth said) and was soon in tears also.[5]

Children suffered not only in the commercial establishments, which included factories, mines and workhouses, but their social status in family set-ups was also downgraded. Pip in *Great Expectations* is quite depressed even in the house of his elder sister. He lives like a slave; every moment is a terror to him. Mrs. Joe was cruel and authoritative. Pip reveals:

> I was always treated as if I had insisted on being born in opposition to the dictates of the reason, religion and morality and against the dissuading arguments of my friends. Even when I was taken to have a new suit of clothes, the tailors had orders to make them like a reformatory and no account to let me have the free use of my limbs.[6]

The novels of Dickens are replete with hard facts of the miseries of children. David, Pip, Nell, Dick, Oliver and Paul are not only the suffering little heroes of his novels but are also the true representatives of the tormented children of the Victorian age.

Appalling Conditions of Prison Houses

Another aspect of the social evils of the day portrayed by Dickens is the appalling conditions of the prison houses. The need for the reform of prisons is stressed through pictures of squalor and dirt, drinking and gambling, sorrow and suffering. Prisoners were insufficiently clad and were not cared for. In fact, Dickens personally experienced the uncongenial condition of prisons when he was a child and used to visit his father who was in Marshalsea prison and later as an active reporter when no aspect of society could escape his notice.

The prisoners were stuffed in single cells under unhygienic conditions. In *Great Expectations*, Pip says:

> All that time the jails were much neglected and the period of exaggerated reaction consequent on all public wrong doing and which is always its heaviest and longest punishment was still far off. So Felons were not lodged and fed better than soldiers (to say nothing of paupers) and seldom set fire to their prison with the excusable object of improving the flavour of their soup. (246)

During his imprisonment Mr. Pickwick remarks that the idlers and rascals hardly seem to mind their imprisonment at all. Sam Weller confirms this observation:

> It's t'other vuns as gets done over, with the sort o' hang them down hearted fellers as can't svig avay at the beer, nor play at skittles neither them as vould pay if they could and gets low by being boxed up. I'll tell you wot it is, Sir, them as is always a workin wen they can, it damages too much."[7]

No wonder that Mr. Pickwick can bear no more the squalor, the noise and the turmoil: "I have seen enough. . . . My head aches with these scenes and my heart too. Henceforth I will be a prisoner in my own room." (645)

In *David Copperfield* and *Little Dorrit*, Dickens gives a vivid description of the prison life and in part this emphasis is simply another manifestation of his life-long preoccupation with prisons.

Delay in Justice

In the days of Dickens, Doctors Common did the work that was later taken by Probate Court. The same judges dealt with the naval and religious matters. Dickens could never understand why experts in ecclesiastical law should be considered competent to deal with nautical affairs. He made the interesting discovery that human nature on oath in the witness box is displayed in its most variable and therefore funniest moods. He rightly concluded that the most useful period of his life was spent as an observer at Doctors Common.

Dickens saw intense suffering around him. The widespread poverty of masses of people sickened him but he wanted to make his case against causes rather than results. The focus of injustice in England seemed to him to be the very organisation, which was established to remove injustice. Obviously the law, in its ideal intent should aid and protect individuals but as legal institutions had developed in England, they had grown into an inextricable mass of red tape and inefficiency.

Mr. Bumble in *Oliver Twist* rightly describes the law as an ass, an idiot beyond the law courts, the lawyers, and the technicians of muddling procedures.

The best example of delay in justice is seen in the novel *Bleak House*. The great lawsuit of the book is the classic case of Jarndyce and Jarndyce, as the lawyer Kenge remarks, "the monument of chancery practice":

> In it every difficulty, every contingency, every masterly fiction, every form of procedure, known in that court is represented again and again and in the court costs have already amounted to between sixty and seventy thousand pounds.[8]

Dickens comments that the principle of English Law is business only: "Let them but once perceive that its grand principle is to make business for itself at their expense and surely they will cease to grumble." (555)

Abuse of the legal system and delay in meting out justice are also criticised by him in *David Copperfield.* In the novel, we get a detailed account of the working of the Courts of the Doctors

Common. Spenlow and Jorkins are selfish lawyers who exploit the legal machinery for their own benefit. They have entered the profession to earn money and they freely exploit the ignorance of the people to further their own ends. And through such pictures, Dickens succeeded in focussing attention on the many abuses of the legal machinery of his day.

Haves and Have Nots

Money is the main theme of nearly every book that Dickens wrote. Getting, keeping, spending, owing, bequeathing provide the intricacies of his plots. Character after character is constructed round the attitude to money. Social status without it is subordinate.

Money is the instrument by which a villain thwarts the hero and the two are chiefly distinguished by their attitude towards it. Money is a weapon of immense power. Physical strength, passion, religion—all quail before it. Dickens has a far more acute sense of what money can do for those who have none than of what might be done with it by those who have plenty. His good richmen have no style beyond kindness, no taste beyond comfort.

Giving security and happiness to a few people for their lifetime is more important than providing a public endowment that might last for generations. His interest in the haves is almost confined to what they can do personally, good or evil, to the have nots. The proper heroes and heroines are those who suffer and are helped.

This glorification of the underdog cannot be attributed to Dickens's personal experience in the narrow sense that he suffered agonies of shame for his early poverty. *Oliver Twist* is governed more by the acquired opinions and attitudes of adolescence and early manhood than by the discussions of the Poor Law.

People's minds were then focussed upon the facts and problems of poverty. That is why when Dickens wanted to show his benevolent reformism in action, he started at the poor men's end. Close observation of poor people at home and laying out their wretched income prepared the way for generous intervention. For instance, in *Old Curiosity Shop*, we are shown first the inner details of the Nubbler's household:

> rocked herself upon a chair wringing her hands and weeping bitterly but Kit made no attempt to comfort her and remained quite bewildered. The baby in cradle woke up and cried, the boy in the clothes basket fell over, on his back with the basket upon him and was seen no more; the mother wept louder yet and rocked faster. But Kit, insensible to the entire din and tumult, remained in a state of utter stupefaction.[9]

In fact, one of the reasons why Dickens's benevolent sentiment still has the power to bring tears to the eyes is that he has so carefully and realistically built up the scenes of poverty, depression and unhappiness, that the ultimate release, the death, the £ 5 note, the turkey, the job and the smile, bring a break of tension also for us.

All the good characters who can afford it are great spenders. They pay good wages, lend on generous terms and give large amounts away. We are not allowed to forget that Christianity must lead to practical benevolence needing a lot of money.

Defective Parliamentary System

Dickens became a press reporter in the House of Commons in the spring of 1832 when the Reform Bill was going through the Parliament and the mass of Englishmen believed that the country was shortly to be transformed into a paradise. Having heard the nation's representatives and noted the effect of their deliberations, Dickens came to the conclusion that an average politician was a windbag, a flunkey and a self-seeker and that triumph of any party merely benefitted a class. Parliament was a spectacle of noise and confusion, shouting and roaring and shameful turbulence. There was no system, no harmony.

Parliament reform had not accomplished much that Dickens regarded as valuable, nor would it, he was convinced, as long as the aristocratic industrialists and the rich merchants controlled the parliament.

In *Bleak House*, he lashes out, though very humorously, at the political corruption of the Chesney World. Sir Leicester Deadlock's conversation with his cousin Volumnia about the general election and his horror that his housekeeper's son (a good industrialist) has been invited to go into the parliament, are as effective as the satire of Chancery Lord Boodle's after-dinner conversation with Sir Leicester:

> Supposing the present Government be overthrown, the limited choice of the new ministry would be between Lord Doodle and Sir Thomas Coodle then giving the home department and the leadership of the house to Boodle and the exchequer to the Koodle, the colonies to Loodle and the foreign-office to Moodle. What are you to do with Noodle? What follows that the country is shipwrecked, lost and gone to pieces because you cannot provide for Noodle? (174)

This appears a good fun but we have critics like Bernard Shaw declaring that Dickens's penetration of our party system with its Coodle, Doodle Foodle etc. has never been surpassed for accuracy. He is quoted with approval by Edgar Johnson who agrees that this can hardly be allowed to pass. It has been built into a conception of Dickens as a profound social prophet attacking the forces of greed and privilege spinning their labyrinth-web of corruption in modern England.

Dickens had been sympathetic to the Chartist programme of suffrage, vote by ballot, annual parliaments, abolition of property, qualification for election to parliament and division of the country into equal electoral districts. He agreed with Carlyle's declaration in a thick pamphlet entitled Chartism that the movement voiced protest against a social organization, dominated by privilege and wealth.

Slums

In most of the novels of Dickens, we find a clear delineation of the foul areas of St. Giles and Saffron Hill and the slums of Whitechapel, Rotherhithe and Bentham Green. With hideous realism, he painted the squalid shops of Field lane, flaunting the silk handkerchief bought from pickpockets, the piles of old iron and bones and stolen clothes rusting the rotting in grimy heaps. Almost every novel of Dickens presents scenes of slum areas. Worse than the slums presented in *Oliver Twist* and *Pickwick Papers*, is the urban slum of Tom All Alone:

> A black, dilapidated street of crazy houses, tumbling down and wrecking with foul stains and loathsome smells, dripping with dirty rain and shattering with its ruined wall a human vermin that crawls and coils itself to sleep in Maggot numbers on the rotting boards of its floors among felig-rags.

Further

> Twice lately there has been a crash and a cloud of dust like the springing of a mine in Tom All Alone's and each time a house has fallen. These accidents have made a paragraph in the newspaper and then filled a bed or two in the nearest hospital. The gaps remain and there are not unpopular lodgings among the rubbish. (232-33)

In *Household Words* the articles on sanitary reform and slum clearance are so many. Statistical analysis demonstrates that the most crowded slums have the highest mortality rate.

> Health by act of parliament arguing for London's inclusion within the Public Health Act quotes figures to prove that the monetary loss in the metropolis caused during the year 1848 by typhus alone was £ 440,000.[10]

Cholera however is the most spectacular of many preventable diseases caused by polluted sewers, bad or insufficient water and several other articles gird repeatedly at the incompetence and negligence of the public bodies supposed to deal with these matters.

Industrialism

In the Victorian age, the industrial revolution of the age transformed the agrarian economy of England into an industrial economy. Mills and factories were established and the whole of England hummed with the rattle of machines. The industrial revolution created a new class of privileged mill owners and big industrialists, rolling in riches. It also brought in its wake the semi-starved, ill-housed and ill-clad class of labourers and factory workers whose rights were yet to be protected.

National wealth increased but it was not equitably distributed. A new class of landed aristocracy sprang up and it looked at the lot of the ragged and miserable factory hands with eyes of disdain and contempt.

Conditions of life held no charm for the labourers and the workers in the field because they were required to dwell in slum areas with no amenities of life.

Dickens's novels contain some very realistic pictures of the wretched lives of the miserable poor. His novel *Oliver Twist* displays scenes of squalid life in London slums. *Hard Times* is an unveiled attack on the contemporary political economy of the school of Gradgrind who is the chief protagonist. It is a satirical exposure of the evils of industrialism and worship of machinery. Coketown is described as a town of machinery and tall chimneys out of which unending columns of smoke rose upwards forever and ever. Dickens writes: "It was a town of unnatural red and black like the painted face of savage."[11] The employers never realize the need for any relaxation or physical relief. In fact, the workmen are not men at all. They are hands who have to work for satisfying the material lust of their employers:

> The men who make money through the labours of these hands regard the smoke of the chimneys as meat and drink for the capitalists. Any sympathy for the workmen is, regarded by the capitalists as humbugging sentiment. (22)

The industrial town represents industrial ugliness, industrial callousness and the monotonous life, which the workmen are compelled to lead under a system of utilitarianism and laissez-faire. All the passages, which describe the town or its people, are written in an ironical vein and have an obvious moral purpose.

From the above discussion it is revealed that the novels of Dickens were not written at random but, instead, his attention was always focussed and arrested with some reformatory target which he achieved successfully.

Similarly the writings of Premchand were not swayed with emotional idealism only, but were always fraught with the stark realities of the social problems. However, the various parasites, afflicting the contemporary rural India and which Premchand deeply intended to eradicate, can be summarized as follows:

Dowry

During the period when Premchand wrote, the marriage tradition of Hindu society had become so polluted and hopeless that any reform seemed nearly impossible. Very rarely could parents welcome a daughter, even if she was born after seven sons. One reason for this was that the rate of dowry was increasing disastrously. And as a result, some parents were compelled to marry their young daughters to old men. Some were forced to die in agony and desperation and there was no scope of having an equal match.

Due to the curse of dowry, Suman, the heroine of *Sevasadan* is married to a widower, Gajdhar Prasad. Similar is the case of Nirmala who is married to Tota Ram of 40 years.

Some social reformers used to speak very eloquently against dowry but when their own turn came, they forgot all about their preaching. And Premchand was not unaware of this. In his story "Ek Anch ki Kasar," he satirizes such parents: "Sahib! we hate dowry. It is against our principles. But what to do? The children's mother does not agree at all."[12]

Premchand abhorred dowry but he reveals here how under various pretexts, parents accepted the same. Sweeping out all the doubts, he clears the tendency of the time:

> Nirmala is pretty, talented, intelligent. She belongs to a prestigious family but let her be, if dowry is there all blemishes transform into merit. Qualities have no worth, only dowry has value."[13]

He reveals that all the defects are counted as merits if dowry is there. Many other examples can be quoted where Premchand wishes to uproot this blood-sucking curse of dowry.

Helplessness of Widows

Apart from dowry, another cause of suffering of Indian women was the helpless condition of widows. A widow had no right to the income of her husband. So, in a joint family, she was tortured. Even the parents of widows were not willing to accept her. Ratan in *Gaban* is a striking example of this. She is the wife of a rich advocate. He loves her ardently and is always ready to fulfil her every desire. While he is alive, Ratan spends a very luxurious life without any restrictions. But after the death of her husband, everything is finished. Manibhushan, the nephew of her husband, deceives her badly and sells her property without her knowledge. She is ruined. She wails:

> I have told you. I have no relation with anything in this house. I was just a mere hired servant. What relation a hired maid has with a family. Oh, who was the sinner who formulated this law! . . . If I had enough strength, I would have made my voice reach the whole country and called upon all the ladies, "Sisters, do not get married at all in a joint family, and if you do so, don't relax unless you have built a house of your own. Don't think you will be honoured in that house after your husband's death. . . .You cannot escape humiliation and destitution. . . . A joint family is not a bed of roses but a couch of thorns. It is not a boat, which will sail you to the shore. It is a huge beast, which will swallow you."

The force of circumstances urges her to reach out to all the women-folk in the country and warn them against the fallacy of getting married in a joint family, which would ruin every prospect of happiness and peace.

Rukmani, the widow in the novel *Nirmala*, takes shelter in the house of her brother Tota Ram. However, Tota Ram does not look after her like a member of the family. He says to Nirmala:

> Oh, I always thought that she is a widow, just an orphan, she needs a little bit to eat. When even servants are eating here, she after all, is my sister. Besides I required a woman too, to look after my children. That is why I kept her here. But it does not mean at all that she should dominate you. (62)

It shows the thinking of a real brother who feels that a widow sister has no right to interfere in his family affairs. Phoolmati in "Bato Vali Vidhva," after the death of her husband, finds no soft corner in the hearts of any of the members of her family.

Thus, we see that Premchand championed the cause of widows and wanted to better their conditions.

Superstitions

Superstitions had gripped the society of the times. There was a belief in the existence of ghosts and witches. For the illiterate and orthodox people of India, it was very difficult to believe in the dictates of reason.

In the story "Balidan," Girdhari Lal commits suicide on the same day when he sells his bullocks and after the death he becomes a ghost and begins to hover around his field.

In "Suhag ki Sari," Gaura does not want to throw her bridal sari in the Holi of foreign garments. She feels that this sari is a symbol of her Suhag and just to throw it into the fire, would be an ill omen.

In the house of Damodar Datt (Tetar), a daughter was born after the birth of three sons. (A child born after three sons or daughters is called Tetar.) And it was believed that such a child would prove very unfortunate for parents as well as for himself. Mother of Damodar Datt says to him: "Because of Tetar only, your grandfather expired. Since then my heart quivers as soon as I hear the name of Tetar."[14] It shows that superstitions were prevalent and "Tetar" was considered an ill omen and a calamity. Consequently the innocent daughter is tortured but still she remains alive. Through the fourth child of Damodar Datt, Premchand attacks the fallacious superstitions existing in the society. The son scoffs at the superstition and refutes all such beliefs:

> Mother, this is all a hoax. Have Tetar girls never existed in this world or that parents of all Tetars have died? (115)

Corrupt Police Force

In *Premashram,* Premchand throws light on the functioning of the police:

> Before making a decision in any case whether it is true or false, it is imperative that the testimony of witnesses is properly appreciated and, on that basis, an opinion is formed. However, the police officials tread in the reverse direction. They first form an opinion and then try to find witnesses and proofs to justify their decision.[15]

Premchand strikes at the investigation made by the police in the novel. When messenger Gausakha of Lakhanpur village stops the flow of tank water in severe heat, Sukhu Chaudhari protests, along with other peasants, against this tyranny. Consequently, Gausakha becomes the enemy of Sukhu Chaudhari. He imputes a false allegation on Sukhu who receives the hard punishment of two years. Premchand writes:

> Nooralam raided the village, Sukhu Chaudhari had never tasted opium nor had he even seen it or heard its name. But 10 gms. of opium was recovered from his house. No sooner was the drug seized than he was taken into custody. (349-50)

It reflects how police implicated innocent persons. Further, in *Karambhumi*, about the corruption of Police force, Gaznavi says:

> If the government can ever reform police, the demand for independence can be postponed for fifty years. Today nobody wants to be in touch with police. Police station is considered a resort of hooligans. This is a black spot upon the government.[16]

Gaznavi accuses police and its misdeeds. This accelerates the demand for independence.

The reality was that Police used to patronize theft and dacoity. After taking bribes, they let the rich tyrannize the poor. Not only this, but sometimes to grind their axes, they entangled even innocent people in a false case and others for purchasing stolen goods.

Prostitution

Gandhi said that prostitution is very pathetic and insulting. In order to appease the sexual desires of men, women have to prostitute their prestige. He said that for the way in which women have been degraded by men, they will have to suffer a severe punishment. In *Godan*, Premchand points out two reasons for prostitution: (i) lack of honour and (ii) economic problems.

Dr. Mehta and Mirza Sahib always have discussion on this issue. Mirza Sahib comments:

> Only those women come into prostitution who do not get honourable shelter in the family due to some reason or those who are economically depressed.[17]

But Mehta has a different view: "Chiefly, the inherent desires and physical lust attract the women towards this profession." At another occasion, Mirza Sahib says:

> And I again affirm that this is a question of mere survival.

He insists that it is due to the economic compulsions.

Further, Premchand mentions that society is not ready to accept these fallen women. Very patiently, Suman of *Sevasadan* stays in the Widow House, but when widows become aware of her past, they don't like to live with her. About Suman, the in-charge of the Sadan comments:

> She pretends to be pious. She is posing chastity after committing all kinds of sins. A statue of god can never be reconstructed once it scatters into pieces. Even if she becomes a goddess, I will not believe her.[18]

Through the in-charge of Sadan, Premchand reveals the thinking of the society, which refuses to accept a fallen woman.

No doubt, Premchand feels man to be responsible for this evil. As Johra says in *Gaban*:

> Excuse me, sir, you are siding with the men. The bare fact is that you go there for lust and sensual pleasure, just to forget your present. If you do not go there in search of true love, how can you get it at all?[19]

She defends prostitution, which thrives on money. The element of love has nothing to do with it. Men go to prostitutes only for recreation.

Moneylenders and the Pitiable Conditions of Farmers

Moneylenders, in the Premchand era, used to lead a very luxurious life. They always had opportunities to suck the blood of farmers because most part of the production was finished in grainyard.

In "Sava Seer Gahun," Vipra lends to Shankar, a farmer, one and quarter seer of wheat. But within seven years, this amount reaches to twenty-five kg. and Shankar has to write a document of sixty rupees. But Vipra asks for fifteen rupees more for which he cannot arrange. And as a result, he is forced to work on the field of Vipra, for half a seer of barley daily, a blanket and a shirt every year. After slavery of twenty years, Shankar dies but he still has debt of twenty-one rupees on his head for which his son has to pass a similar life of slavery.

Dhania, the wife of Hori in *Godan*, has experienced it very well in her married life of twenty years:

> Howsoever economic one is, even if every single penny is saved and calculated, escape from tax is impossible. (1)

There was no Mahajan in the village from whom Hori had not taken debt. This condition was not only of Hori but also of most of the farmers.

After taking debt once, the farmer remained in the clutches of the Mahajan always. Hence, the labourers and farmers were depressed. They were never debtless and just to keep them alive, some quantity of grain was given to them. Their wages were eaten in interest. And a big amount was deducted towards commission.

Untouchability

Varnashram Religion was founded in ancient times. Later, its form was distorted. Hindu society was divided into castes and subcastes. The result of this was that most serviceable class of society was devoid of all economic, political and religious rights and this untouchable class remained Hindu only in name. Premchand, in his several short stories and novels, gave vivid pictures of such untouchables.

Since long, Jokhu of "Thakur Ka Kuan" is sick. The water which his wife brings to drink has bad smell. She thinks that some animal has died in the well. By having such water, Jokhu will be more sick. But it is quite impossible for her to take water from somewhere else. She feels:

> Who will allow us to take water from the Thakur's well? Sahu's well is also at the other corner of village. But nobody will allow us to carry water from there too and there is no other well in the village.[20]

It throws light on the miserable lot of untouchables who were not allowed to go near the wells of Caste Hindus.

Such inhuman behaviour has been discussed in *Karambhumi* also. In Thakur Dwara (temple), a holy recitation has been going on for one month. Some untouchables also begin to listen to the story of Thakurji. But when Brahamchariji comes to know about it, he gets annoyed: "These rogues used to come to the temple daily and people used to take prasad touched by them. What could be worse than that?" (199) Here is reflected the contempt for the untouchables due to the belief that even if they touch the prasad of God, it becomes impure.

On one side, untouchables were object of such hatred, and on the other, those belonging to Hindu society preached to bring them on an equal level. But when their own turn came, they refused.

Untouchables used to do all the cleaning work. In villages where nurses and lady doctors were not sufficient, the daughters and daughters-in-law of untouchables used to do all labour jobs. Besides this, beautiful maidens of untouchables remained the objects of lust for unscrupulous rich men. Even after so much service, they were not allowed to enter the houses of the so-called high-class people. If some kind-hearted man permitted them to do so, he instantly became the object of criticism.

Bribery

Tendency of taking bribes was prevalent in every class of government workers, which enabled people to pass a life of comfort and luxury. Those who did not take bribes, their subordinates were displeased with them because it was a great hindrance in fulfilling their own selfish aims. The fact was that every body was aware of this corruption. Lala Samarkant in *Karambhumi* says:

> There are so many senior officials. Tell me, who does not take bribe. If you want to get a copy of any statement, you have to offer a bribe of one rupee. Without getting his commission, the policeman does not even register a complaint. (45)

Premchand lashes at the corrupt bureaucracy and even its high officials where even the police are not an exception. Ramakant in the novel *Gaban* is a servant in a corporation. He takes bribes from businessmen and when his father asks, he replies: "Commission is not a bribe. All accept it. People offer it without my asking for it. I don't demand it from anyone." (52) Bribe had become a way of life and everybody accepted it as a necessary evil.

Breaking up of Joint Family System

In the rural economic system, there was the importance of joint family. This system taught the family members to work selflessly. Everybody had an assurance of livelihood. In the field of consumption, there was great saving and things were accomplished on comparatively less expenses. In joint family, the best use of money was possible and land could be saved from division and sub-division.

Despite all these benefits, joint families were disintegrating. In the novels of Premchand, we have several references to this. The story *Algyojha* has this theme. In *Godan*, due to the grudge of Hira, two brothers separate. Hira gives poison to the cow of Hori and runs away. At such a time, Hori has to look after Punia: "Prestige and honour of the whole family is always one and undivided. Who can ever dare to go against it?" (31) Premchand says that although in the joint family system, family disputes were not uncommon, whenever some outsider tried to intervene, the prestige and honour of family was considered uppermost.

Hira starts the tribulations in the life of Hori. These are followed by such a long chain of troubles that he is never able to recover himself. On the one hand, joint family system symbolized mutual cooperation; on the other, it became the cause of perpetual hatred and jealousy in the same families.

Strange scenes of envy, anger and hatred were seen among the women. And this trend was not limited up to them only. The things reached the ears of men and separation resulted.

In *Godan*, Malti, while going with Mehta, visualizes that the joint families are breaking due to rift and envy. This division distorted the whole rural economic system. One person cannot bear up the burden of fields. The only way to increase the earning was debt and a peasant never flourishes under the yoke of debt. Thus the economic complications increased due to the breaking up of joint family and led to the misery of farmers.

Reaction to Various Evils

In a society affected by these problems, Dickens and Premchand came forward as the true representatives of their respective ages. The age of both the writers was the age of conflict and great commotion. Their novels give a clear idea of the prevailing evils and their reaction against them. Their hearts are with lower and lower middle class. Most of the heroes and heroines of their novels are from this suffering class.

Everywhere Dickens saw the conditions, which aroused indignation. He walked at a vigorous pace, sometimes by day, sometimes by night, through the crowded areas, and observed the filthy congestion and the inadequate water supply, which resulted in disease and crime. He decided to strike a blow against these evils. Dickens saw how hoodlums and corruption inevitably sprouted from the very cobblestones. Only fundamental changes could strike at the root of the evil. "How radical I am getting," wrote Dickens to Forster in August 1841. "I was stranger and stranger in the true principles every day."[21]

All his writings from *Oliver Twist* to *Our Mutual Friend* make it clear that Dickens was not advocating tyrannical authority. In all his novels, he set out to attack some specific abuse in the existing system of things and throughout he adopted the role of a champion of the weak, the outcast and the oppressed. In *Oliver Twist* (1833), he showed that the Poor Law Reform Act had only strengthened institutionalism by giving authority to unkindness. In *Nicholas Nickleby* (1939), he exposed what was going on behind the doors of public schools. *Bleak*

House (1853) is a sombre story of hearts worn to despair and minds driven to madness by the inscrutable injustice and the infinite delays of the law. In *Hard Times* (1954), Dickens attacks the industrial evils of the day. The target in *Little Dorrit* is the unreformed civil service with its nepotism and injustice.

Although he could see with clear eyes the stranger impersonal evil created by society, he continued to believe in the kindly fatherhood of God and in the triumphant power of love. Organization, whether political or charitable or religious, he rejected; the law killed and any system, no matter how efficient, was no substitute for the warm human relationships that were based on man's responsibility for his fellows.

Similarly, Premchand also raised his protesting voice against existing evils, religious orthodoxies and superstitions. His sympathetic heart always overwhelmed for the poor, helpless and downtrodden peasants.

In his first novel, *Sevasadan*, he attacks the social evils of prostitution, dowry, and unequal matches. Premchand in fact does not react against these social curses but the reasons which are responsible for such traditions. In *Karambhumi* and *Gaban*, his target is the government servant taking bribes. In *Rangbhumi*, he attacks the conflict between the rural and the urban life as well as the selfish landlords. *Godan* is against those moneylenders and capitalists who are responsible for the suffering of poor farmers.

Premchand not only attacks these evils in his writing but also puts forward several solutions. In his novels and short stories, we get the hints to solve the problem of dowry:

1. The parents of the bridegroom and the bridegroom himself should renounce the greed of dowry.
2. Young girls should have the strength and courage to refuse such selfish men.

Further, to improve the position of farmers, Premchand gives following suggestions:

1. Forced labour from farmers should not be allowed.
2. The tradition of taking bribes should be ended.
3. The monthly income of the landlords should be raised so that they do not exploit the farmers to fulfil their necessities.

For the solution of the problem of prostitution, Premchand suggests:

1. There should be some arrangement for the livelihood of these helpless women.
2. Marriages of unequal matches should be prohibited.
3. If some prostitute falls in true love, she should be helped to get married.
4. The evil of prostitution should be completely abolished. For this, proper arrangement should be made for the marriage of the daughters of prostitutes.

Thus, it is apparent that Dickens and Premchand attacked not only the existing systems, but also the forces working behind them. Although both of them had a vision to eradicate the social evils in the national interest but their ways to eliminate them differed. Despite so many common grounds, they approached the problems in different ways. Similarities and dissimilarities are apparent in their cultural environments and their childhood.

Similarities between Dickens and Premchand

1. Both Dickens and Premchand were brought up in the shadow of poverty and destitution. They protested against the prevailing evils, not because they were conscious about them

as a writer of social novels but they themselves had suffered this agony which was later on depicted in their novels.

2. Both were champions of middle and lower middle-class and they depicted the problems and ethics of this class. Their sympathies are with those who are struggling for better days. In almost all their novels, the protagonists belong to middle or lower middle class, who always win our favour.
3. Both lived in an age when industrialization and urbanism were raising their ugly head and in their wake reared many social evils. They not only protested against these but also visualized a utopian exemplary society in which these evils would have no role to play.
4. Both were against capitalism and its effects. Their ardent desire was that the poor get their due share in the national income and the whole wealth is not concentrated in the hands of a few capitalists.
5. Prostitution was one of the hard curses of the times of both these novelists. So many women, deserted wives and young maidens, fell a prey to this degraded profession. Both Dickens and Premchand raised their sympathetic voice against these fallen women. They emphasized that society should accept them, arrange for them and give them an opportunity to renew their life.
6. One more striking resemblance which exists between the two is their strong protest against the administrative circle. Dickens wrote against the inefficiency of law, delay in justice and defective parliamentary system while Premchand could not spare the corrupt police force, its greed, its selfish and opportunistic trends. He also lashed such government workers who took bribes to grind their own axes.

Dissimilarities between Dickens and Premchand

1. Although the objects of sympathy of these novelists were the poor and the downtrodden, Premchand was more concerned with rural life, with the problems of farmers, villagers, landlords and moneylenders while Dickens always dealt with the urban problems of an industrial city.
2. The novels of Premchand are concerned with the problems of women: child marriages, unequal marriages, dowry and prostitution. But in the age of Dickens, England was a progressive country. The social status of the women and their role in national affairs was on far better footing than in India. Hence the women characters in the novels of Dickens are not so depressed and grief stricken. Instead, they are quite intelligent, conscious of their womanhood and quite decisive.
3. Children in Dickens's novels are the most miserable victims of society and Dickens seems to be acutely concerned with their betterment. Since he himself had passed through this ordeal in his childhood, his pen always cried for the suffering children. But India, at that time was an agricultural country having joint family system. So the child was not a problem for Indian peasants. The growth of industry was also very slow, so labour problem was not so acute. Under these circumstances, Premchand's mind was not occupied with child upliftment.
4. During the time of Premchand, India was fettered in the shackles of dependence. But when Premchand started his literary career, the flame of freedom had already been kindled. England was exploiting Indian resources and looting its wealth, expanding its treasure at the cost of India and proudly exploiting its colonial sovereignty. India was smarting under economic depression, illiteracy and tyranny

of English Crown. Premchand was inspired by national spirit. In all his novels, he can be seen striking hard at this exploitation. But in the novels of Dickens, this element does not exist at all.

NOTES

1. Edgar Johnson, *Charles Dickens: His Tragedy and Triumph* (London, 1953), p. 8.
2. George Orwell, *Discussions of Charles Dickens*, ed. William Ross Clark (America, 1959), p. 36.
3. Charles Dickens, *Oliver Twist* (England, 1966), p. 58.
4. Charles Dickens, *Nicholas Nickleby* (England, 1968), p. 235.
5. Charles Dickens, *David Copperfield* (New York, 1957), p. 89.
6. Charles Dickens, *Great Expectations* (New York, 1953), p. 20.
7. Charles Dickens, *Pickwick Papers* (New York, 1959), p. 576.
8. Charles Dickens, *Bleak House* (New York, 1853), p.36.
9. Charles Dickens, *Old Curiosity Shop* (New York, 1957), p. 81.
10. Charles Dickens, *Household Words* (London, 1969), I, p. 352.
11. Charles Dickens, *Hard Times* (New York, 1955), p. 22.
12. Premchand, "Ek Anch Ki Kasar," *Mansarovar II* (Allahabad, 1969), p. 90.
13. Premchand, *Nirmala* (Jaipur, 1965), p. 55.
14. Premchand, "Tetar," *Mansarovar II*, p. 109.
15. Premchand, *Premashram* (Allahabad, 1969), p. 167.
16. Premchand, *Karambhumi* (Allahabad, 1965), p. 3.
17. Premchand, *Godan* (Allahabad, 1960), p. 329.
18. Premchand, *Sevasadan* (Variance, 1962), p. 230.
19. Premchand, *Gaban* (Allahabad, 1972), p. 287.
20. Premchand, "Thakur Ka Kuan," *Mansarovar I* (Allahabad, 1970), p. 142.
21. John Forster, *The Life of Charles Dickens* (New York, 1966), II, p. 135.

The Social Purpose of Dickens and Premchand

In any form of art or literature, particularly with a social objective, two elements are always prominent: the collection of matter and the undercurrent of feelings which enliven it. Yashpal, a significant Hindi writer, has said: "A true artist of literature cannot fulfil his social obligation and feel elated merely by eulogising beauty and chivalry. It is also incumbent on him to conjure the sense of the development and perfection of society as well as by invoking the enthusiasm of people and to make them conscious by their analytical powers."[1]

When we go through the works of Dickens and Premchand, one thing, which strikes us, is that their novels have been written to present before us the contemporary conditions with which they were not satisfied. In their works, they realistically portrayed the picture of their times.

One can call Dickens a romantic realist because there is an element of romance in his novels. Comparatively, Premchand is a social realist. In his works, imagination has taken the form of idealism. There is not much exaggeration of facts in his novels which appear more realistic than those of Dickens in which idealism is easily achieved and takes the form of romanticism. However, both of them wanted to present the real thing before the reader to which they have given different colours of their own.

The English novel before Dickens had either sought for romance in the lives of highwaymen or in haunted ruins and gothic castles. In Dickens's hands, English novel returns once again to the contemporary life of London. But his is not a mere photographic reporting. His subject is real but it is heightened and glorified by his creative imagination. It is in this way that the common is made uncommon. There is a blending of realism and romance, fact and fiction, truth and fantasy in his novels.

Hugh Walker rightly calls Dickens "the romancer of London streets and slums."[2] He depicts contemporary London; its squares, its busy thoroughfares, its noise and squalor, the neat and tidy cottages have all been pointed out in detail. There is a constant ordering and selection of material till we get a heightened and idealised picture of reality. The coarse and crude is thus softened and more pleasant aspects are emphasised.

Further, his imagination fastens upon human oddities and eccentricities. Many of his characters have been based on real human beings; but their peculiarities of dress, manner or speech have been much exaggerated. He omits the unpleasant and disgusting and still gives us reality.

In *Martin Chuzzlewit*, Mrs. Gamp is a character of the most delicate idealism. She is a sick nurse, in life loathsome and vulgar but in Dickens's novel, a source of endless amusement. In life, she is revolting. In Dickens's delightful company, she is at once typical and individual.

In his novels, Dickens looked at the world through the eyes of little children and described the people as children would describe the grown-ups. Thus Steerforth becomes David's hero and Betsy Trotwood his fairy Godmother.

Another reason, which makes Dickens's world fantastic, is that in the interest of poetic justice, the good is always rewarded and the vicious punished in the end. Justice is often tempered with mercy. In doing so, Dickens often exaggerates the facts.

Thus in depicting the real facts of his age, Dickens has given them a garb of his own imagination and fantasy. On the other hand, Premchand is neither a blind follower of the old or of the new. As a writer, he expresses his feelings in his own way, according to his age. He selects his plots from every walk of life. The prominence of truth and reality is always noticeable in his writings. About his plots, he wrote to Dr. Madan once:

> I construct my plots according to what is aesthetic and relevant in human character. It is a highly mysterious phenomenon because sometimes I get inspiration from an individual or from an incident or from some dream but human psychology always remains the basis of my writings. Though I give a tinge of imagination to my characters, most of them are from real life.[3]

Premchand observed different aspects of human life from a different perspective. Whether it is a town or a village, politics, history or religion, in his novels we find a very realistic presentation of all these. His novels depict the so-called lower, middle and higher classes. There is no dearth of women like Suman who had to accept a degraded life due to circumstances or of men like Gajadhar who assist in the fall of society. Neither the Pandits like Matadeen and Datadeen are missing who have affair with a Chamarin, Silia, but still do not hesitate to rob the innocent villagers in the name of untouchability. The farmers like Hori struggle all through their life due to their simplicity. Sometimes, there is a protest against injustice done by the Government officers. At other times, there are accounts of their sorrow-stricken lives.

Thus, both Dickens and Premchand wrote for their people, about their respective ages. Both had a purpose behind their writings. To fulfil this, they always gave a real picture of their society. However, no writer can create real art unless its ugliness is partly distilled. Both Dickens and Premchand blended their observations of the glaring reality with judicious mixture of imagination and idealism, thereby lending greater propriety to their artistic manifestations. But the play of imagination is more evident in the works of Dickens than in Premchand and that is why Dickens deserves to be called a romantic realist. Premchand, on the other hand, instead of purely romanticizing, believes in idealising the real. Thus it is preferable to call him a social realist.

Belief in Socialism and Democracy

Premchand always considered an intimate relation between literature, society and politics. To him, literature was a reflection of contemporary political circumstances. In his age, there sprouted an unprecedented awakening and political consciousness. The emergence of Mahatma Gandhi on the political scene gave a new turn to Indian politics. Under his leadership, two major movements were launched between 1920 to 1931. These were: the Non-cooperation movement of 1921 and eight years later the Salt Satyagraha. Premchand was also enthralled by these two movements. His conscience groaned for democracy and he gave vent to his feelings in his novels and short stories.

There is a clear impression of Gandhian philosophy on the personality of Premshankar in *Premashram.* He devoted himself entirely to the service of farmers. Due to his simplicity and honesty, the life pattern of so many gamblers, drunkards and tyrannous government officers is changed.

Surdas in *Rangbhumi* is the most successful and living Gandhian character. Though physically weak and miserable, he has immense power of soul. He decides to protest against the despotism not by the force of weapons but by the power of his conscience. He says to Bharo:

> if the government has the power to kill, we have, if nothing else, the courage to die.[4]

This is apparently the Gandhian policy of non-violence. Amrit Rao says that Surdas is an ideal Satyagrahi, not in the limited sense of political movement but in the larger sense of life as a whole.[5]

Although Premchand did not actively join the field of politics, he disclosed quite successfully the secrets of those selfish classes, which always proved a hindrance in the way of national movement. Landlords were afraid to give any movement the form of political movement because at any time the British government could implicate them for having waged a war and could confiscate their property. Kunwar Bharat Singh of *Rangbhumi* wants to serve his people unless it affected his property. Dr. Ganguli could not believe in such pseudo national feelings:

> Now you must have came to know why we don't trust the rich. They are mere slaves of their wealth. They can never plunge into the battle of truth. A warrior with a gold brick around his neck can never fight in the battlefield. (543)

Throwing light upon the imperialistic policy of the government, the English District Magistrate, Mr. Clark, says:

> The British empire wants to keep India as her integral part. Whatever party it may be—Conservative or Liberal, Radical or Labour—all of them cherish the same ideal. The English have never been known for sacrificing their lives for a higher cause. They are imperialistic. (389)

He discloses the policy of English empire famous for its colonial expansion irrespective of whatever party is ruling.

Premchand was an ardent supporter of socialism. He observed the social arrangement of his age very minutely. The life values were changing and developing vigorously. Industrial and economic trends were given the name of capitalistic civilization. Premchand writes:

> This is the glory of this age. There is no value of a human being. What is important is money and machine. And this is responsible for the disintegration of villages and the scourge of cottage industries.[6]

In *Karambhumi*, Premchand protested against the economic gulf between the rich and the poor:

> If one person can live on ten rupees, why does the other require ten thousand rupees? (122)

He lashes out at the economic differences in the society.

At several places we find him criticizing this difference and feeling that capitalism is, to a very large extent, responsible for this. He wished for an economic system where everybody would have equal share in the economy and which would completely uproot slavery and poverty.

When we turn to the works of Dickens, we find that both these elements are subservient in them. Dickens belonged to the greatest democratic nation but in that era of industrial revolution, democracy was not functioning well with an imperial crown on its head. Long before Dickens, parliamentary system had been introduced. Although like his own contemporaries, he wanted welfare legislation to be passed but nowhere do we find him criticizing the democratic pattern, perhaps because he knew that England, being a democrat at home, was clinching her despotic grip over the colonial regime and was continuously following the expansionist policy in respect of her foreign affairs. India was one of the preys of English hypocrisy and Dickens nowhere mentions this exploitation. But how could Premchand remain immune to this when everyone in India was crying for democracy?

Moreover, England at that time was becoming richer through rapid industrialization, which brought in its wake the economic inequality, a new class of capitalists emerged. No doubt, Dickens always groaned for his suffering countrymen. He always tried to share their pains. He was aware of the sparse diet given to a pauper, the miseries of those poor children who were subjected to hard labour and punishment before they became able to observe the cruelties of this world. He was also conscious of the fact how money under the impact of industrialisation poured into the pockets of rich people.

All these aspects have been delineated boldly in his novels. But in his works we feel the absence of any protest against the lack of socialism. About the socialism of Dickens, George Orwell comments very frankly:

> The truth is that Dickens' criticism of society is exclusively moral, hence the utter lack of any constructive suggestion. He attacks the law, parliament, government, educational system and so forth, without ever clearly suggesting what he would put in their place. . . . There is no clear sign that he wants the existing order overthrown or that it would make very much difference if it is overthrown. [7]

Although both the writers are champions of the poor class, the spirit for democracy and socialism is more striking in the works of Premchand. This was due to the contemporary political and economic conditions, in India, which was a dependent country at that time. But Dickens belonged to a democratic country, which was exploiting other countries, and he did not raise his voice against this exploitation.

Evolutionary or Revolutionary

We have already observed that the age of both the writers was of rapid political and social upheavals. And they could not isolate themselves from the grievances of their countrymen. In the heart of their hearts, they wanted a definite change in political and economic sphere.

In Dickens's time, the breach between the rich and the poor was increasing. The poor were struggling. The overbearance of poverty and depression were awakening a protesting spirit inside them. Edgar Johnson comments:

> In this way Dickens bears locked within his memory the hidden reproach of the debtor's prison and the blacking warehouse but he shares in his heart the despair of those victims of the workhouse 'Bastilles', feels the miseries of emaciated toilers, condemned to hard labour in factories like jails, has experienced the anguish of wronged and deserted children. Can such evils ever be righted, such sufferings ever be expiated? Can the Bastille-prisoner ever be recalled to life. Can the past with all its dreadful weight of guilt and pain ever be bottled out? Will not wrong generate wrong flaming into all the horrors of the revolution engulfing both innocents and the guilty in a sacrificial cataclysm?[8]

This is what Johnson remarks as a critic of *A Tale of Two Cities,* the central theme of which is politics. The main impression of the novel is the horror and bloodiness of the revolutionary atmosphere and the grim idea of vengeance, epitomized in Madame Defarge. The novel is an expression of Dickens's own impatience and anger in his identification with those slaughtered mercilessly. The concentration of emotion in the novel is on the wild frenzy of people who have committed everything to violence.

There is sympathy with the frenzied victims of oppression, turned wolfish that rises into a fierce exultation. But Dickens never favoured any revolutionary change in contemporary social or economic system. His criticism was never harsh. Being a writer of middle and lower middle class, he wished for a reform but this reform he desired always through evolutionary means.

The age of Premchand can be said as a revolutionary period. Resentment with foreign rule which started in 1857 was becoming more intensified. Although the oppressive policy of British rulers was doing its work with full momentum, the reaction to this policy was becoming visible in new forms. The writers, through their literature, presented society and a person in their chosen garb. Besides resigning his job, Premchand contributed through magazine articles and editorial comments to the awakening of people. He lent his full support to the non-violent way of freedom. In his story "Lal Feeta," he favours all the aspects of movement. Daily processions were being taken out. Sometimes, people did not approve these. In the story "Jail," Mridula speaks in their favour:

> People often ask what is the use of taking out processions. Well, they prove that we are alive and that we are undaunted.[9]

Processions may not be able to achieve anything substantial but these nevertheless remind the oppressors that man is a living organism.

In his novels Premchand has created several Gandhian characters, expressing his full devotion to the policies of Gandhi. Premchand favoured the fire of freedom, but he had obvious doubts if violent revolution could contribute towards the welfare of the country. He wrote in *Hans*: "They may deem themselves victorious after killing two or three workers but it is difficult to assess the harm they are doing to the nation." This establishes Premchand's antipathy towards revolutionary measures.

Both Dickens and Premchand wished for certain reforms and urgent changes in the social framework of their countries but nowhere in their works do they state that such a change should be through violent and destructive ways. Rather, they wanted the reforms and changes to come peacefully.

As Champions of Have Nots

It becomes evident from their biographies that both Dickens and Premchand had drunk that cup of sorrow and suffering which filled their whole life with such a bitterness that they could not resist giving expression to it in their works. All through their novels are expressed the sordidness and pains of life, which they suffered and became successful in awaking the conscience of the people and becoming the champions of have-nots.

In England, the aristocracy was domineering in every field. Industrialism and capitalism were completely ignoring the cause of the lower classes. Poor were becoming poorer. There was darkness, desperation, misery, helplessness and disappointment around them. The gulf between the haves and have-nots was becoming hard to fathom.

The new Poor law fostered by the Utilitarians was intended as a reform. But Dickens thought it to be a wrong step. The Benthamites argued that there ought to be work for everybody and a man out of work deserved little relief. Therefore they prescribed such conditions as to make the workhouse as bad as possible. Conditions in England during this period of industrialisation were such that a large number of labourers was condemned to pauperism for life and once a labourer became a pauper under the new system, his home ruthlessly broke up.

Apart from the ugly conditions of workhouses, Dickens attacks the poor law and pauperism in his novel *Oliver Twist*. Oliver is brought before the board who set him for picking oakum in the workhouse. Then follows the famous scene in which Dickens describes the pauper's diet and Oliver asks for more. Immediately an animated discussion takes place. The next day he is taken to the hall where the boys dined and were socially flogged as public warning and example. At last when Oliver gets an apprenticeship in Mr. Sowerberry's undertaker's shop, he pushes him down a steep flight of stairs into a damp and dark stone cell, where he is given some of the cold bits of meat the dog has not taken.

Dickens always called the attention of the reader towards those who had been crushed down by the cruel hands of destiny--destiny in the form of cruel administrators who never cared for underdogs, rolling on the streets and asking for justice. In his novels, we find true depiction of lower classes of have nots, of slum dwellers and paupers, of poor children and helpless prisoners.

Premchand was also upset by the social status of common man. Conflict between rural and urban life drew his attention. He saw the poor peasants, their lifelong poverty, their hard labour and their hearts full of sacrifice. He also observed the tyrannies of landlords and moneylenders. Most of the middle classes were earning either by agriculture or by services. In services also, they were poor subordinates to their bosses. In villages the poor were tyrannized by landlords and in cities by harsh capitalists.

In his novels, Premchand speaks for the cause of those who do not have and against those who cause them not to have. He championed the interests of the poor. His *Premashram* and

Godan are regarded as the epics of the peasants's life. Virjan, in the novel *Vardan*, lives in Majh village and writes in a letter to Kamla Charan:

> Oh, what a discrepancy between what I heard and what I am seeing. The scenes of dilapidated huts, muddy walls, heaps of garbage in front of houses, filthy buffaloes—all these make me wish for leaving this place at once. Look at the people: they are in a deplorable condition. Even their bones are devoid of flesh and are clearly visible. They are reincarnations of poverty, wearing worn-out clothes. So unfortunate are they that they do not have enough to eat even after toiling throughout the day.

Here is depicted the lamentable condition of villages as well as of the poor and unfortunate villagers who seem to be the living examples of poverty.

When we observe the life of Hori in *Godan* we realise the deficiencies of the farmer life. He works hard day and night but does not get milk or ghee even for anjan. In her 36 years, his wife has developed wrinkles, her hair is white, and her eyesight is weak. For her three sons who are unwell, she cannot buy even medicine. She had nothing but a small blanket to save Hori. from the severe cold:

> In his childhood, he used to sleep with his father wrapped in this blanket. In young age, he spent his cold nights with Gobar in the same blanket. Now in old age this worn-out blanket was his companion. But now it was not like the teeth with which he could eat food, it was like an aching tooth. There was hardly a day in his life when he could save something after paying the taxes and to the moneylender.[11]

No doubt the traditional land system was fully responsible for this miserable condition of the villagers. Landlords and their messengers were exploiting the interests of poor farmers. In *Premashram*, this tyranny can be well seen where not only the farmer but every villager has become its prey.

To sum up, in the works of both the writers, there are clear pictures of misery and poverty, frank impressions of the protests by the poor against the forces, which were giving eminence to riches. The two writers always sympathised with the miserable sufferers of their respective countries. And there is no exaggeration in calling them the champions of have-nots.

Social Reformers

No doubt, there was a definite purpose in the writings of Dickens and Premchand. In his own day, Dickens was regarded as a radical. As Gissing points out: "Dickens's radicalism consisted in a profound sympathy with the poor and boundless contempt of all social superiority that is merely obstructive."[12]

Dickens was constantly aware of the wide gulf between the rich and the poor. He was distressed to find the privileged section of the society thriving on the toils of the impoverished majority. His only wish and hope was to strike a blow for the poor and these blows he did strike right manfully. Many of the social ills came under the lash of Dickens and through his writings he represented the dissatisfaction of the common public against these evils.

But we should not ignore the fact that Dickens is as much a realist as an optimist. He is never tired of emphasising that moral virtue is to be found in all classes of people irrespective of birth and education. He does not consider the poor from any level of social superiority. His attitude is not one of patronage but of equality.

Dickens fights the battle of the poor in his own way. He entertains his readers, captures their attention and then makes them think. He was that rare type of reformer who could moralise with a smile and mix his sermonic powers in such an excellent way that his contemporaries did not realise that he was doctoring them for their good.

And when we come to view the works of Premchand, the fact that strikes us is that he did not consider literature as the mirror of society only but a means to enlighten its way. Premchand believes that the only difference between Neetishastra and literature lies in their creation. Both Neetishastra and literature aim at the development and reform of life. While the medium of Neetishastra is reasoning and preaching, literature prefers psychological considerations.[13]

Premchand's themes are taken from all walks of life. He was not only a keen observer but also a great creator who first measured his period and then gave his message. He was aware of the fact that due to the impact of western civilization there was great struggle between the old and the new in the contemporary society. In every field of life, there was an attempt for rejecting the old social values and cultural measures and giving them new social and timely forms.

Premchand depicted not only the various problems in his work but also at several places his suggestions reveal how minutely he had peeped into the facts of life. He thinks parents to be responsible for a successful alliance:

> How negligent we are towards our domestic life! We don't feel any need to prepare and educate our girls. A girl who plays with dolls and enjoys with her friends is considered competent to get married. It is like an immature calf bearing the burden of a heavy yolk. No wonder, our family life is not peaceful.[14]

The statement shows that Premchand was a keen observer even in the spheres of domestic affairs. Further he writes in *Godan*:

> Marriage is a social agreement. Neither man nor woman has a right to violate it. You are free before entering into this agreement; later, things get beyond your control. (61)

Premchand attacks religious orthodoxies and frauds of priests and also the policies of selfish landlords and moneylenders. He writes about the corruption prevalent in administration and also about the limited rights of various departments.

Both Dickens and Premchand were inspired to write such things which may benefit those people for whom they wrote, by ringing the buzzes for people, who had no capacity to reach their voice to their cruel administrators, and this is why they are called social reformers. Although they were neither the political leaders nor the heroic soldiers of the battlefield, yet their contribution was not less because they were the mouthpieces of the common man whose condition they always wished to ameliorate.

Firm Believers in Art for Life's Sake

Literature is a thing of heart because it depicts various feelings of heart presented with the help of imagination. However, it is neither a playground of fantasies nor an excited creation of mind. In fact, it is a true picture of the development of our thoughts. Premchand writes in *Kuch Vichar*: "The highest ideal of literature is that it should be created for the sake of art. None can object to the principle of "Art for Art's sake." Only that literature can be eternal that is based on the instinctive elements of life like envy and love, anger and greed, devotion and detachment, sorrow and humiliation. The basic aim of literature is to depict them. There can be no literary creation without a purpose." (45)

Premchand believes that perfect art is that which is created not only for the sake of art but for life's sake as well, in which basic emotions of human beings are present illustrating the spirit of time.

When we view the works of both Dickens and Premchand in this light, we find that they did not present a purely romantic picture of life but tinged it with realism also. There is a happy blend of art and morality in their work.

Dickens never departs from his duty of teaching a moral lesson. While the virtuous are rewarded in the end and made happy, the wicked are punished. In *David Copperfield*, Dickens writes in the last chapter:

> And now the written story ends; I look back once more for the last time before I close. . . . I see myself with Agnes at my side, journeying along the road of life. I see our children and our friends around us; and I hear the roar of many voices not indifferent to me as I travel on. (876)

Similarly, in *Oliver Twist*, Harry Maylie proposed to Rose and was accepted. Fagin was tried and sentenced to death. He went mad in jail. Mr. Brownlow took Oliver and thus at last he came into his long inheritance. In *Great Expectations*, although all the expectations of Pip had come to nothing yet he had got something more valuable than money and that is the experience of life. In addition to this, Pip and Estella are brought together. Pip at last is united with his dream girl.

Thus Dickens gave a happy and appeasing ending by rewarding the virtuous. In his preface to *Oliver Twist*, Dickens asks why the dregs of life (as long as their speech did not offend ear) should not serve the purpose of moral? This indicates two limitations of his realism:

1. He could not be realistic in the speech of his characters. He could not represent a foul-mouthed person speaking in his natural manner.
2. His characters are made subservient to his moral purpose.

Thus he idealises reality. George Orwell writes regarding the morality of Dickens: "His radicalism is of the vaguest kind and yet always knows that it is always there. . . . All he can say is behave decently." (44)

Dickens is always on the side of underdog. To carry this to its logical conclusion, one has got to change sides when the underdog becomes an upperdog and in fact Dickens tends to do so. He loathes the Catholic Church, for instance, but as soon as it is really presented (*Barnaby Rudge*) he is on its side. He loathes the aristocratic class even more, but as soon as they are overthrown (revolutionary chapters in *A Tale of Two Cities*) his sympathies swing round.

Comparatively, Premchand is more realistic. Most of his characters meet the hard end of life. They see suffering around them and, despite their honesty and simplicity, pity is not showered on them. However, Premchand was not a supporter of crude realism. Through Chakradhar of *Kayakalp*, he speaks: "Realism is adorable but the bare reality is abhorable."[15] Nevertheless, he is conscious of the danger of mere idealism. He writes in *Kuch Vichar*: "If Realism opens our eyes, then idealism takes us to a heavenly place. But while idealism has this quality, There is every danger that such characters may be created who are mere idols of principles." (43)

According to Premchand a successful writer should present art with realism and idealism, but he should be careful that his idealism should not be a flight of imagination only. In his early novels, his idealism sometimes crosses the bound of reality or probability. In *Sevasadan*, for example, there is quick reform in the characters of Gajadhar and Suman. *Premashram* appears more realistic than *Sevasadan*.

Premshankar in *Premashram* is an ideal character and he has returned from America wishing to establish an ideal agricultural society. After the establishment of Premasharm, he succeeds in bringing even the evil characters to the noble ways of life. In the end, the evil characters are either reformed or murdered. Here, Premchand appears to be moralising.

In his next novel, *Nirmala*, the problem about unequal matches is discussed. In the end, the whole family is destroyed. Two sons of Tota Ram die, the third one runs away form home. Tota Ram also flees away. At last, Nirmala gives up her life.

Critics have considered *Nirmala* as one of the most realistic creations of Premchand. Ramdeen Gupta says: "*Nirmala* is the first realistic tragedy of Premchand where he has not suggested any idealistic solution. The writer of *Nirmala* concentrates on the analysis of the problem and not its solution. This is the reason why the story does not lose itself in the maze of idealism but briskly moves towards its cruel but reasoned ending."[16]

In *Rangbhumi* also, he shows the real conflict between rural life and industrialisation and the final victory of urbanism. In this novel, his idealism is quite practical. In the words of Shanti Kumar:

> I am not an idealist. I have more experience of the world than you. I have repeatedly experimented in my life and reached the conclusion that compromise is the basis of our life. You may think whatever you like but a time will come when your eyes will open and you will realise that the importance of realism is not a whit less than idealism.[17]

The statement throws light on the views of Premchand who always felt that in life the importance of realism is not less than idealism. And in his last novel, *Godan*, he has proved that for the class differences, for the exploitation and miseries of exploited class, not any individual tribe or class but the whole social order is responsible.

Thus, art for both the novelists was not for art's sake only. They loved those flowers which bring fruits, they loved those clouds which shower water. They could love beauty not only for its own sake but for the sake of life. They are romantic in their conception but realistic in their treatment.

No doubt, idealism and realism existed in both the novelists, though in different proportions. On several occasions, we find them moralising through their characters. But in this respect, Dickens is ahead of Premchand. Poetic justice can be seen in the works of Dickens. Although idealistic characters appear in his works also, but his themes are more real and his moral or idealism is more practical.

Both Dickens and Premchand wished to convey profound meaning to their people. They wrote for the society, and their novels reveal the society itself. Being social reformers, they always wished to uproot the curses and frailties of the society.

NOTES

1. Yashpal, "Ek Vaktavaya," *Desh Drohi* (Allahabad, 1978), p. 8.
2. Hugh Walker, *The Literature of Victorian Era* (London, 1973), p. 472.
3. Madan, *Premchand: Ek Vivechan* (Delhi, 1968), Parishisht 2, Letter 2 (6).
4. Premchand, *Rangbhumi* (Allahabad, 1965), p. 465.
5. Amrit Rao, *Kalam ka Sipahi* (Allahabad, 1962), p. 311.
6. Premchand, *Vividh Prasang*, Part II, p. 496.
7. George Orwell, *Discussions of Charles Dickens*, ed. William Ross Clark (U.S.A., 1961), p. 31.

8. Edgar Johnson, *Charles Dickens: His Tragedy and Triumph* (London, 1953), II, p. 974.
9. Premchand, "Jail," *Mansarovar* (Delhi, 1970), III, p. 14.
10. Premchand, *Vardan* (Allahabad, 1955), p. 90.
11. Premchand, *Godan* (Prayag, 1960), p. 118.
12. George Gissing, *The Works of Charles Dickens* (London, 1910), p. 247.
13. Premchand, *Kuch Vichar* (Banaras, 1955), p. 3.
14. Premchand, *Sevasadan* (Varanasi, 1962), p. 98.
15. Premchand, *Kayakalp*, p. 153.
16. Ramdeen Gupta, *Premchand Aur Gandhivad* (Delhi, 1961), p. 223.
17. Premchand, *Karambhumi* (Allahabad, 1965), p. 111.

The Technique in the Novels of Dickens and Premchand

Charles Dickens and Premchand delineate social problems in their novels in a deft way. To obtain a comprehensive view of their stature, it is desirable to give due consideration to the technical aspects of their writing. As we turn to their technique of plot-construction, characterisation, style, humour and pathos, we find that their novels are not only manuscripts of social problems but also such presentations that can be relished by men of literary taste.

Plot Construction

Premchand has a vast range for his plots. The initial analysis of the life situations and the sentiments and functions of characters make the end of the situation seem quite explicit. In *Kayakalp*, Manorama says: "If I were the queen of Jagdishpur, I would give you a lot of money without your asking for it." And then Chakradhar says: "I will remind you of this sometime."[1]

The conversation between Manorama and Chakradhar indicates the probability of her becoming the queen of Jagdishpur—an aspiration that is ultimately fulfilled. Premchand is an ideal novelist who believes in portraying realism but is careful to abstain from the use of pornographic touches in his novels. Suman in *Sevasadan* and Munni in *Karambhumi* are placed in uncongenial circumstances but Premchand cleverly avoids any undesirable portrayal. He has created both heavens and hells in his novels, but peeping into his hell gives no feelings of detestation.

Premchand's plots are from various walks of life. The plot of *Sevasadan* revolves around the conservative infirmities; in *Premashram*, he tells us about the conflict between farmers and landlords. Its range is wider than that of *Sevasadan*. In *Rang Bhumi*, it is still wider. Here, apart from Hindus, Muslims and Christians, political disputes, beggars, gods and priests are also present. *Karambhumi* is about untouchability, *Gaban* about corrupt police force.

In spite of some artistic flaws, there is an unbroken flow in the plots of Premchand. In the novel *Nirmala*, Kalyani says:

> Ever since Brahma created the world, none has ever been able to please the wedding guests. One, who cannot afford a dry loaf of bread at home, claims to be a lord in the wedding party. There are thousands of complaints, i.e., the oil is not scented, cheap soap is provided, the attendants do not properly attend to you, the lanterns are smoky, the chairs have bugs, the cots are loose and the wedding place is not airy enough.[2]

The various complaints made by the bridegroom's guests in the bride's place reflect the keen observation power of Premchand.

Sometimes, there is repetition of incidents in the novels of Premchand. However, whether these incidents are new or old, their development is always natural. Even the abstract incidents of *Kayakalp* are arranged in such a manner that they do not seem unnatural. They are co-related and seem to sprout from the main story and develop around it, and give a cumulative impression on the mind of the reader.

Dickens, however, is not known for his plot-construction. His plots, except for the last two or three novels like *A Tale of*

Two Cities, *Barnaby Rudge* and *Edwin Drood*, are incoherent and lack unity. Indeed, as Walter Allen says: "His early novels are like shapeless bags which contain something for everybody and parts of which one does not can more or less be ignored."[3]

As a matter of fact, with the exceptions mentioned above, the plot is the weakest part of Dickens's novels. His plots are not organic wholes. The crudities and improbabilities of his plots are astonishing. Often his plots are subordinate to character. We remember his characters because they are so charming but often we cannot place them in the novel to which they belong.

Gissing rightly points out that Dickens's plots do not grow out of plausible human situations. He never learned the art of adapting simple probable events and situations to the end of narration. He further comments: "Too often the novelist prefers some far-fetched eccentricity, some piece of knavishness, some unlikely occurrence around which to weave his tale."[4] This fault can be seen in *David Copperfield* and many other novels which followed. This weakness as well as his use of the melodramatic is explained by his fondness for the stage. Another weakness of Dickens's plots arises from the fact that he could never acquire the art of "skilful revelation of circumstances, which for the purpose of his story, he has kept long concealed."[5]

Moreover, the closing scenes in his novels are always unnatural and forced and Dickens's narration frequently suffers from much tedious superfluity. Frequently, he opens a chapter with a long passage of old-fashioned moralising which has nothing to do with the story. In *Martin Chuzzlewit*, there is a long chapter directed against the advantage of high birth, which is entirely superfluous, and the story would gain much by its omission.

However, the above faults may be accounted for in a number of ways. Much that is conventional in Dickens's plot results from his fondness for the theatre and picaresque tradition.

Moreover, he often wrote against time and the rapidity of production tended to looseness of construction. The serial method of publication had this further disadvantage that he could not see mentally the whole of the work on which he was engaged, and could not make alterations in the earlier incidents even when he considered such alterations necessary. Besides, he always cared more for the character than for the plots or incidents. As David Cecil puts it: "Dickens may not construct the story well, but he tells it admirably. With the first sentence, he grips the attention of the readers and does not let it go till the very end."[6]

Thus, we can say that the device of plot construction of the two novelists was different. Premchand was definitely superb in this regard. However, we should not forget that whatever be the ways of conveying their art, it was art with a purpose. Their aim as a social reformer was to focus on the contemporary problems. Although Dickens could not achieve the height of technique, especially in his early novels, he succeeded as a social reformer, which was his main purpose in writing the novels.

Characterisation

Going through the various novels of Dickens and Premchand, we feel that the most important fact about Dickens's art of characterisation is the immense variety and vitality of his characters. Indeed, here is God's plenty. His Micawbers and Peggottys, his Betsy Trotwoods and Uriah Heeps are amazingly vital. However, Dickens's art of characterisation suffers from a number of limitations.

Much of the unreality of Dickens's characters arises from the necessities of plot. Dickens could not create probable and plausible situations. Thus, in *David Copperfield*, boatman Peggotty is a lifelike and convincing character but who can put faith in him when he sets forth to search for his niece in the highways and byways of Europe.

Such a situation does not arise in the case of Premchand. J.P. Jha Dwij feels that Premchand is always aware of the mutual contrast between plot and character. His novels have a proper mixture of these. His characters reveal themselves through the progression of events in the plot. Situations and characters cannot be seen in isolation since they are complementary to each other.[7]

Suman in *Sevasadan* accepts prostitution due to the circumstances she is in. In *Gaban*, Ramanath steals the ornaments of his wife under economic pressure and pilfers money from his office. Being a victim of circumstances, he becomes the architect of the inhuman conspiracy against innocent people and is compelled to live a life not of his choice. But he has absolutely no say in making or marring his destiny.

In Dickens's characters, there is heightening and idealising of reality. To quote Gissing: "The harsh is smoothed, the worst of everything is forgotten, things pleasant come into relief." (108) Mrs. Gamp in *Martin Chuzzlewit* is a piece of the most delicate idealism. She is a sick nurse, loathsome and vulgar in real life but a source of endless amusement in the novel.

In the works of Premchand, both idealism and realism are present but such a heightening of reality is rare. In his novels, the influence of situation is unpredicted. In *Kayakalp*, Chakradhar, who was once ready to sacrifice even his life to save the life of a cow and was the most true and humble comrade of labourers, assumes the mannerisms of the haughty rich when he starts living in luxurious environment even for a brief period. When the farmer refuses to push his car, he says: "Get lost or do I slap you? People like you do not listen to words." (415) Circumstances have converted the gentle Chakradhar into a rude person. Due to this incident, Chakradhar becomes very much depressed. He understands its root cause: "Living in such atmosphere [being a ruler of the state], it is impossible for me to control my instinctive desires. Money has religion, pity and large-heartedness. But it also has pride which ruins all other virtues." (430) Similarly, in *Godan*, the hero Hori dies a very pathetic death. Premchand could have given some comforting turn to his end, but he is aware of the conditions of a farmer and does not want to falsify the fact.

In general, Dickens delights in presenting external peculiarities of his characters. He gives us a vivid picture of the externals but he is not good at the analysis of character. His characterisation is only skin-deep. He describes the physiognomy, manners and habits of the characters rather than give us a glimpse of what goes on within their minds. His characters are flat; they do not change. Dickens attached a label or trademark to his characters and sometimes we find it difficult to recognize the characters if their trademark is missing. Such for example are the humbleness of Uriah Heep and the chronic buttonlessness of Peggotty in *David Copperfield.* Dickens's genius is for the extensive, not for the intensive vision and so he has tried to portray the infinite diversity of men and women in his novels. We think of a Pickwick or a Sam Weller, a Jingle or an Oliver Twist, a Smike or a Micawber, a Peggotty or a Pip or a David Copperfield. Their diversity brings out the essential features of human beings.

However, such limitations are not there in the novels of Premchand. He is a master of psychology: "Amarkant wanted to embrace Sakina and pulled her close. That very moment, the door opened and Pathanin entered. Sakina retraced her steps. So did Amar."[8] Premchand's poignant portrayal of the intense feelings of young lovers in *Karambhumi* amply demonstrates his psychological insight.

In comparison to the characters of Dickens, those of Premchand are more vivid, lively and closely related to the plot. However, the characters of Dickens cannot be labelled as mere caricatures. Gissing comments: "That is why his characters even when exaggerated have immense life and vitality. They are unforgettable." (165) Dickens looks at people through the eyes of little children. His greatest success lies in the portrayal of the eccentricities of his characters. The humorous, eccentric and abnormal characters helped him in achieving the purpose of his art.

Humour

In their novels, Premchand and Dickens present life in its various forms. They delineate the elements of anger, hate and laughter. Both the writers were great humorists not only of their respective periods but also occupy a prominent position in their fields.

Humour was the supreme quality of the genius of Dickens. It was the very soul of his works. Humour in Dickens underwent a gradual evolution. In his earlier works, it is broad and farcical—an expression of the hilarity and irresponsible gaiety of youth.

The wild absurdity of the Muffin Company in the beginning of *Nicholas Nickleby* is a farce in a boyish mood. Later on, Dickens uses this extravagance to soften the bitterest of truths. The scene between little David Copperfield and the waiter serves such a purpose:

> A dish load of cutlets is set before the poor starving boy. The waiter eats it up and tries to make the people believe that it is the boy's achievement.[9]

Dickens makes us laugh and then compels us to think. Our sympathy is aroused for the poor suffering creatures like David.

True humour is illuminating; it results not in broad laughter but in thoughtful smile. Both Tony and Sam Weller are humorous creations. After knowing them, we know ourselves better. We smile at the quaint philosophy of Old Weller. Sam, still young and at ease with the world, makes life a jest and we cannot help laughing with him when he sees so shrewdly and feels so honestly. The satire may be exaggerated but it is always based on reality.

Dickens's humour is very rich in those passages, which serve as illustrations of manners than of individual characters. No one has equalled Dickens in bringing out the humour of stupidity. One of his masterpieces in this connection is Old Weller, the landlord of Maypole. He has a high notion of his importance. He does not talk much but asserts his dignity by a blank stare of imbecile resentment of which the very Gods would stand fixed between amazement and laughter. Simpletons, even idiots, in this way become objects of humour. Humour often arises from their sublimely idiotic talk.

Humour and satire are present in a very steady and static flow in the novels of Premchand. Laughter arises on appropriate occasions and it gives rise to beauty and grace in proportional ways. Premchand writes:

> Humour should be devoid of obscenity and malice. Literary humour is different from social humour. The same thing which evokes laughter in a social gathering becomes a matter of criticism in literature. Stories of Khusro and Birbal are quite hilarious but bringing most of these into literature will be an insult to literary taste.[10]

While Dickens glorifies the humour of stupidity, Premchand believes in exercising definite restraint on the quality of humour. He draws a clear line between those situations which give rise to laughter and those which he deems presentable according to literary standards.

In *Pratigya*, his first novel, Premchand has not lost any opportunity to entertain us. When Kamla Prasad, the son of a rich miserly person, brings two silk saris, one for his wife and one for Purna, it creates doubt in the mind of Sumitra:

> It seems that you have hit a jackpot. Tell me the bare facts. Whom have you cheated? You cannot buy such useless things with your hard-earned money.[11]

Premchand shows very humorously that even the wife of a miser cannot believe that her husband can bring a sari from his own pocket. In response to the constant nagging by his wife, Kamla Prasad irksomely retorts: "I have broken the safe in your father's house. Where else could I go to commit a dacoity." Sumitra refuses to tolerate this taunt and starts praising the generosity of her father: "If you had asked for money, my father would have given you the sum. There was no need to break the safe." (50)

Premchand often mixes satire with humour in a superb way. When Kamla Prasad and Deena Nath go to watch a film, Kamla Prasad comments repeatedly:

> Look, here is Chaplin. Wow. He is a match for you. Oh, what are you looking at? Look at this lady. I swear I am ready to serve her if she keeps me as a servant to do even menial work like fetching water. Wow. Such fairies still exist in this world. And look at our country. Oh wretched, are you sleeping? (50)

Here Premchand depicts the frivolous mentality of people like Kamla Prasad who lose their mental bearing on seeing a beautiful woman.

Gluttons and misers have always been a source of laughter in literature. In *Nirmala*, Premchand has pictured the condition of Pandit Mota Ram thus:

> Fidgety with greed, he was very impatient. Sweets worth one anna had crushed his hopes already. And now this delay also. He was really helpless. (81)

Premchand elicits laughter by exposing the greed of the pandits. Sometimes his humour conceals a deep meaning behind it. In *Premashram*, Mirza Sahib has opened a community orphanage and collects charity in its name. But spending a luxurious life, he is always in debt. He has instructed Maulavi Sahib that he should tell the creditors that he is not home. But somehow when one succeeds in coming, he scolds Maulavi Sahib that he should have pushed him aside. But this is intolerable for Maulavi Sahib:

> Sir, dry bread and thin dhal do not have so much energy. How can I fight if I do not get enough to eat. Lying on the threshold, I merely smell spices and tasty food.[12]

Premchand satirises the selfish people like Mirza Sahib who pretend to be very charitable but at home even their subordinates are not satisfied with them and do not get enough to eat:

> At the dining table, I pine for good food. If you serve me that, I will take care no one dares enter the house. (240)

Pathos

Inseparable from the gift of humour is that of pathos. In fact, both Dickens and Premchand knew how to touch and melt. Their imagination is familiar with common sort of human suffering and so they succeed in their purpose of focussing attention on the sad plight of poor victims.

Pathos is indeed one of the predominant features of Dickens's fiction. And it has been rightly pointed out that Dickens greatly excels in pathetic scenes. The several death scenes in Dickens's novels constitute Dickens's most concentrated appeal to tears. Moreover, such scenes have symbolic significance also. The death of the heroine of *Old Curiosity Shop* is symbolic of premature close of a delicate and innocent life. Little Nell typifies the suffering of those helpless children who were then being tortured in English mines and factories in thousands. Dickens writes:

> She was dead. No sleep so beautiful and calm, so free from trace of pain, so fair to look upon. She seemed a creature fresh from the hand of God. She was dead. Dear gentle, patient noble Nell was dead.[13]

The description of Dick is full of pathos, who is aware that he is dying and longs for death because "I dream so much of heaven and angels and kind faces that I never see when I am awake." (55)

Again, Dickens's memories of childhood made him conscious whenever he dealt with the squalid prison world. Much of it centres round the suffering of prisoners in the wretched prisons of the day. There is the death of chancery prisoners in *Pickwick Papers* and an important scene marked with genuine pathos in *Bleak House* is also connected with imprisonment for debt.

Very often, Dickens inextricably blends pathos with humour. The picture of Micawber in the king's bench prisons, with a petition praying for his release spread on the table and other prisoners standing round to read it, is both humorous and pathetic. Indeed, the characters of Betsy Trotwood and Mrs. Micawber are sources alike of humour and pathos. Similarly, the scene of David's first arrival at Salem House is both humorous and pathetic. Little David finds a notice reading, "Take care of him. He bites!" Thinking that there is some dangerous dog around, he climbs the table, but is soon informed that the notice is a warning against him. The picture of little David going around with the notice on his back is both humorous and pathetic.

Sometimes, such scenes are imbued with humanity. The greatest emotional scene in Dickens's novels is the guillotine episode in *A Tale of Two Cities*. The cartoon would substitute for Darnay, provide sympathy and admiration for the hero who achieves nobility by the last effort at atonement for his own previous incapacity. There is no denying the fact that the last scenes of *A Tale of Two Cities* are very effective.

Premchand has also created powerful emotional scenes. There are so many living pictures of moving pathos. Whether the characters are on deathbed or struggling through the thorns of life, they win our sympathy. When in *Godan*, Hori dies working in the severe heat of summer and Dhania is asked for Godan, our eyes are wet:

> A number of voices came, "Yes, let there be Godan [giving away a cow in charity]. This is the right time." Dhania got up mechanically, brought the sum of twenty annas she had earned that day by selling thread. Putting that money in the lifeless cold hands of her husband, she told Datadeen: "Sir, there is no cow or calf or any more money in the house. This is his Godan for his salvation," and fell unconscious.[14]

Our sympathy is aroused with the pathetic scene of Hori's death and we feel the misery of those who are destined to be poor.

Many of Premchand's novels like *Nirmala*, *Sevasadan* and *Rangbhumi* are full of pathos. *Sevasadan* is a story of a beautiful as well as sensible and honest girl Suman. In the grip of destiny, she falls down in such a pit that she finds her salvation quite impossible. Throughout her life, she tries to wash away her sin but even after this contrition, society is not ready to accept her. She wails:

> How unfortunate I am! Even my own sister does not want to see my face. How much I tried to make her my own but did not succeed. I have got a stain on my forehead which cannot be washed off. How can I blame her or anyone else? This is the result of the actions of my previous birth. Oh, I have a great pain in my heel. How will this thorn be taken out? A small piece of thorn is still stuck there and the wound is dripping. No, I cannot blame anybody. I have done impious deeds and must atone for them. Sensual desires are responsible for my present plight.[15]

The pathos is created with the feeling of a beautiful girl who, even after repenting for her deeds, could not win the sympathy of her own people.

In fact, humour and pathos are two inseparable parts of a plot. As our sincerest laughter is fraught with some pain, such pathos enlivens the art. The sadness of our heart merges with that of the character. We sympathise with him, his troubles and tragedies appear to us as our own. In this respect, Dickens and Premchand have much in common as they view life alike through the spectacles of pain and pathos.

Style

Dickens and Premchand had great command on their style. Premchand uses many words of Urdu and English but his language never loses its fluency. In *Gaban*, simplicity and fluency of style is attained through short sentences:

> When the train started moving, Rama felt like crying. It may not be possible to come back at all. These blissful days will never return. They are lost forever.[16]

In *Karambhumi*, there is an excellent illustration of the harmonious blending of experience and expression: "What is the objection? You know my views. This education will ruin our character. We have turned education into a business. Invest more capital, it will result in better returns. Invest more money in education and get a higher position." No doubt, Premchand uses Urdu words in the conversation of Hindu characters. However, we should not forget that, at that time, this was the natural form of language. Many passages in the novels are pure Hindi. In *Karambhumi*, he writes: "A man is a beast to some extent. This beastliness makes him a real man. As per the theory of evolution, he lags behind the woman. The day he achieves perfection, he will turn into a woman." (99) He depends, at times, on the purity of his language in conveying his thoughts and ideas.

The base of fluency and naturalness of his plots is that his plots, characters and situations are finely interwoven. His language suits the various characters. An uneducated Matai speaks thus in *Karambhumi*: "Who will understand the problems of the poor? Whatever you say, you will lose your job. No doubt, all of us are servants. Some are servants of the government, others of the rich." (355) Here is a touching and beautiful expression of the sentiments of the poor and uneducated persons. The truth of feelings makes the style simple, explicit and poetic. There is enthusiasm and sweetness in the following description in *Karambhumi*:

> Like the radiance emanating from the womb of a dark sky, Amarkant felt a ray of light coming out of his inferiority and degradation which endowed his life with a silver glory.

> In the light of the lamps, in the sound of music, in the stars of the sky, there was a glimpse of that infant—his sweetness, his dance. (94)

In expressing the feelings in the depths of human heart, Premchand's style assumes great lyrical power and beauty.

Phrases are the life of language. Premchand's works are full of them. Let us quote here some of his immortal sentences imbued with feelings:

(a) Love is the breeze of spring, jealousy the scorching wind of summer.
(b) Love is the treasure house of energy.
(c) Superb thoughts are the real adornment of beauty.
(d) Child is the toughest test God has designed to assess the worth of a human being.[18]

Premchand puts forth the realities of life in what has taken the form of aphorisms. The foremost reason of the simplicity and naturalness of his prose style is that he never tries to make his simple things to be mysterious. He is always satisfied with the normal beauty of words and also tries to satisfy us.

Dickens has a unique position in English literature for a special form of expression in prose fiction. His artistic method, his choice of material and his manner of rendering that material in fiction is Dickens's style he derived from masters like Smollett, Fielding, Cervantes and Defoe. In his writings, Dickens attempted to prove the techniques used by his predecessors. Dickens was indeed a conscious artist. Discussing Dickens's characteristic style, Lauriet Lane writes: "It is at its strongest organic, at its richest poetic, at its most intense both organic and poetic."[19]

Indeed, Dickens attempted to improve upon his inspiration. His style grows out of the imaginative moment it renders. It recreates that moment physically by every artistic resource of diction, syntax and rhythm. Many of Dickens's phrases like "Not knowing" and "can't say" have grown proverbial. The names like Bumble, Pecksniff, Mrs. Gamp, Bill Sikes and Uriah Heep have become household names. His malapropisms like "reduced counsels" and "patent Brahmins" are quite outstanding. Mrs. Gamp holds forth in all conversation in *Martin Chuzzlewit*: her diction is capable at once of a racy sententiousness and the wildest flights of grotesque imagination and falls into a natural rhythm which too often may be scanned as regular blank verse. Mr. Bumble, Artful Dodger, Fagin, Mrs. Nickleby and Mr. Micawber have a style of native eloquence distinct from everyone else. Dickens has a command over pompous phrases of rigmarole, parliamentary and journalistic claptrap. To be organic and poetic, Dickens's style breaks all bounds of grammatical and verbal decorum. Some critics have objected to this extravagance of style but most of them have accepted it as his eloquence. The foremost purpose of Dickens's style is to satisfy the internal needs of the fictional moment.

Dickens's stories and sketches, especially the later ones, abound in fine dramatic situations of incalculable help to him as a painter of London life. He is at his best presenting the minute details of life. Nothing could be more significant and at the same time grimmer. For example, look at the following description in *Great Expectations*:

> I came into Smithfield, the shameful place being all filth and fat and blood and foam seemed to stick to me. So I rubbed it off with all possible speed by turning into a street where I saw the great black dome of St. Paul's bulging at me from behind a grim stone building which a bystander said was "Newgate prison." Following the wall of the jail, I found the sound of passing vehicles; and from the quantity

> of people standing about smelling strongly of spirits and beer, I inferred that the trials were on.[20]

Gissing observes: "I suppose there is no English writer, perhaps no writer in any literature, who so often gives proof of wonderfully minute observation. It is an important source of his strength, it helps him to put people and things before us more clearly than as a rule, we should ourselves see them." (225)

Dickens and Premchand wrote for the common people. Their approach was not pedantic and they used a simple style in their writings.

NOTES

1. Premchand, *Kayakalp* (Varanasi, 1964), p. 18.
2. Premchand, *Nirmala* (Jaipur, 1965), p. 15.
3. Walter Allen, *Six Great Novelists* (London, 1960), p. 119.
4. George Gissing, *The Works of Charles Dickens* (London, 1910), p. 48.
5. *Ibid.*, p. 31.
6. David Cecil, *Early Victorian Novelists* (London, 1960), p. 31.
7. J.P. Jha Dwij, *Premchand ki Upanyas Kala* (Bihar, 1949), p. 45.
8. Premchand, *Karambhumi* (Allahabad, 1965), p. 174.
9. Charles Dickens, *David Copperfield* (New York, 1957), pp. 76-77.
10. Premchand, *Kuch Vichar* (Varanasi, 1955), p. 48.
11. Premchand, *Pratigya* (Allahabad, 1963), p. 50.
12. Premchand, *Premashram* (Allahabad, 1969), p. 240.
13. Charles Dickens, *Old Curiosity Shop* (New York, 1957), p. 493.
14. Premchand, *Godan* (Prayag, 1960), p. 263.
15. Premchand, *Sevasadan* (Varanasi, 1962), p. 242.
16. Premchand, *Gaban* (Allahabad, 1971), p. 175.
17. Premchand, *Karambhumi* (Allahabad, 1965), p. 99.
18. (a) *Sevasadan*, p. 48; (b) *Gaban*, p. 196; (c) *Rangbhumi*, p. 504; (d) *Kayakalp*, p. 562.
19. Lauriet Lane, *The Dickens Critics* (New York, 1961), p. 12.
20. Charles Dickens, *Great Expectations* (New York, 1953), p. 165.

The Achievement of Dickens and Premchand

Dickens and Premchand highlighted the various parasitic customs which prevailed in the respective contemporary societies. It is undisputed that legislation is the last resort to bring about a change in society; it can entail punitive measures in case of delinquency, but these great visionaries knew that no legislation can bring the desired reform until and unless the conscience of masses is aroused and people are willing to adopt the reformatory legislation. They were aware that until the people know the disastrous facts and results of the innumerable obsolete traditions, no government, howsoever democratic or autocratic, can enforce any ameliorative legislation.

Their achievement lies in the fact that what they visualized was later on adopted by the society through legislation because the government as well as the people felt the necessity of such a legislation at a later stage. Their desired ideals were adopted and the law amended from time to time. Thus, the foresightedness and vision of Dickens and Premchand stand vindicated at last. And herein lies their immortality and universal appeal.

One important aspect concerning minor children in the time of Dickens was the employment of these children in English factories and mines. They were made to work for as many as twelve hours a day. The economic law of laissez-faire held the day and any interference with the individual freedom of contract was regarded as immoral and unjust. Dickens, through various pictures of their suffering, tried his best to awake the conscience of his age. Now we can feel relieved because the law has applied a number of restrictions on child labour.

In general, no child may be employed until he has attained the age of twelve years, which is for the time being the upper limit for compulsory school, or before the close of school hours during which he is required to attend school, or between the hours from 8 a.m. to 6 p.m. or for more than two hours on Sunday or be left to carry or move anything so heavy which is likely to cause any injury.[1] Further, no person under the age of sixteen years may be engaged in street trading as hawking of newspapers, matches, flowers and other articles, playing, singing or performing profit, shoe blacking and other similar occupations.

If a child is employed, in contravention of any byelaws, under any person, to whose act or default any contravention is attributable, the employer is liable to punishment on summary trial. Moreover, if proceedings are brought against an employer, the employer upon information and after giving three days's notice to the prosecution is entitled to have any person (other than the person employed) to whose act or default he alleges that the contravention was duly brought before the court as a party to the proceedings and if after proof of the contravention the employer proves that the contravention was due to the act or default of such other person, that person may be convicted for offences and penalties be imposed.[2]

Dickens has stated in his novels like *Pickwick Papers*, *Great Expectations* and *Little Dorrit* that in any condition prolonged imprisonment is likely to have negative effect on the mind and outlook of those subjected to it. He is of the view that it is the duty of prison administration to transform those committed to its charge into better people.

The main achievement of British Government in this field has been to replace the negative and repressive methods by the positive and constructive ones. "Above all they need to think constructively about what they are going to make of their future, how they can make time serve them instead of serving time."[3] The 1895 departmental committee on prisons envisaged that the task of the prison service should be to release offenders as 'better men and women physically and morally than when they came in.'

The reformatory steps that have been taken in this direction can be summarized as follows.

At one time, the majority of cells in multi-occupation housed three prisoners but in recent years there has been a considerable and welcome shift towards the housing of two prisoners in a cell. Fortunately, it has been found possible for men to share cells with little friction and with no obvious detriment to health.

Much has been done in recent years to improve conditions in the older prisons by modernizing sanitary recesses in cell-blocks and toilet facilities in workshops and exercise yards and by providing modern bathhouses and showers. Sanitary and ablution arrangements in newly built prisons have been designed on modern lines. A high standard of cleanliness is encouraged both in the premises and in the person of inmates. A bath must be taken on reception and thereafter at least once a week. In many prisons, shower baths, which may be used daily, are provided for use. Each cell has a wash bowl and water jug and every inmate is provided with soap, towel, nailbrush, toothbrush and comb. The rarity of epidemics and the absence of evidence of the spread of contagious disease would suggest that the precautions taken are effective.

The messing facilities have been improved. Individual establishments are able to introduce more variety into their menus and the general standard of prison catering compares favourably with that in hospitals and institutions. A catering manager who is a senior member of the staff of the supply and transport branch headquarters has general overview of all dietary matters like kitchen-organization, serving methods and catering staff training.

For reasons of security, it is not possible for convicted male offenders to wear their own clothes. But many years have gone by since prison dress was deliberately designed to be conspicuously recognizable as such. The aim has for some time been to encourage self-respect by improving and modernizing the standard of quality and design of clothing and by introducing more variety. All prison clothing is regularly exchanged for washing and this is carried out at a number of establishments, which have modern well-equipped laundries.

The purpose of physical education and remedial gymnastic is to promote health and fitness, to prevent physical deterioration, to provide opportunity for the acquisition of skills and to ensure that offenders are physically competent to sustain the demands of outside employment. The physical education programme also provides opportunities for inmates to study physical recreational activities. Often, such study may lead towards externally recognized proficiency awards and sometimes it may enable inmates to find jobs after discharge.

The prison medical service has a general responsibility for the physical and mental health of those in custody and a specific responsibility to give advice on any aspect of their treatment, including living and working conditions, clothing and diet. The regular medical and psychiatric reports made on those serving life sentences are of great importance in deciding whether they can safely be released. Apart from this, the facilities of education, libraries and vocational training are provided for prisoners.

Moreover, in each establishment, selected officers are designated to assist inmates in matters affecting legal aid or to appeals. Their task is to identify all inmates who are eligible to apply for legal aid or to appeal or apply for leave, to the court of appeal, criminal division, and to see that they do not fail to do so, through a solicitor about a civil matter or to institute legal proceedings may apply to the Governor for facilities to do so.

The history of prostitution shows that it has two remarkable characteristics. The first is the tenacity with which it persists in civilized communities. The other striking characteristic is the recalcitrance to control.[4]

The long history of prostitution is full of attempts to regulate it and to confine it to certain persons, time and places but a large amount of prostitution has always slipped through the fingers of authority. Severe measures against clandestine prostitution have merely driven it further into concealment.

However since the beginning of twentieth century, conscious attempts have been made to lessen prostitution. These measures fall naturally into two groups: those, which attack the causes producing the demand, and those, which attack the causes, producing supply.

Most of the preventive measures relating to demand are as follows:

Prevention of the sale of pornographic literature, the strict suppression of advertisement of brothels or call houses in the press and elsewhere and in the attempt to separate prostitution from drink and the supervision of premises authorised to sell alcohol.

The other preventive measure usually recommended is that of competing with the prostitute and her employer by increasing opportunities for recreation of other kinds. Clubs and social centres, public libraries and reading rooms, theatres and cinemas, playing fields, swimming pools and gymnasiums help to solve this problem and act as a counter attraction to the public house, the street and the brothel.

Public enlightenment on the subject of venereal disease was and still is hampered by the moral stigma attached to these illnesses. But when the treatment of venereal disease began to be extended and to assume its present importance, the medical authorities realised that in order to combat this form of disease, publicity and propaganda were essential. Venereal disease-clinics and facilities for free treatment are given discreet publicity. The symptoms and effects of the diseases are described in pamphlets, lectures or films provided sometimes by the authorities. Moreover general reforms which aim at improving working conditions for women are also means of preventing prostitution.

The second group of preventive measures consists of those, which aim at preventing prostitution more directly. The most obvious way of this is by attacking the persons who make money out of prostitutes and whose advice and encouragement are so often found to be one of the immediate causes of prostitution. Laws against procurers have now been passed.

But it is not only the activity of procurers, which cause the immediate cause of prostitution. Employment in an occupation, which entails contact with prostitutes or in which opportunities for prostitution abound, may have the same effect. Laws have been passed fixing an age below which women may not work as barmaids, waitresses, hotel chamber maids etc. except with their own family or placing special restriction on the employment of women in work of this kind at night.

Attempts have been made to lessen both the demand and supply of prostitutes. The law and the police, backed by public opinion, are trying to hamper the prostitute's exploiters, preventing them from artificially expanding demand by advertisement and suggestion. Whether they can ever eliminate prostitution is uncertain because prostitution is deeply ingrained in urban civilized life. Thus, prostitution can be reduced only through intelligent and persistent attempts to counteract the caucus which lead upto it.

One more legislative step taken by British Government in regard to social reform is the slum clearance and its redevelopment. According to this, a clearance area is an area to be cleared of all buildings under a clearance order or by a local authority, upon consideration of an official representation or other information in its possession is satisfied in respect to any area i.e., its district—that the houses in that area are unfit for human habitation by reason of their bad arrangement or the narrowness of the streets. Since the most satisfactory method of dealing with the conditions in the area is the demolition of all buildings in it, the authority must cause the area to be defined on a map in such a manner as to exclude from it any building which is not fit for human habitation.

In the housing act of 1957, the term 'house' includes any yard, garden, outhouses and appurtenance belonging there to or usually enjoyed therewith. Once a clearance area has been declared, it is normally the duty of local authority to secure the clearance of the area, either by making a clearance or by purchasing the area and clearing it.

Where a local authority is satisfied in the case of a house or land purchased by or belonging to it within a clearance area not being a house retained by the authority for temporary use for housing purpose that either it is required for support of a house, which is so retained or there is some special reason why it should not be demolished for the time being and the reason is connected with the exercise of the authority's power to retain houses for temporary accommodation, the authority may retain the house for the time being.

Like Dickens, Premchand touched the slumbering conscience of the contemporary masses by raising his voice against the prevailing evil traditions. Among these, child marriage was a malady, which crippled our socio-economic pattern.

According to the census report of 1921, victims of child-marriage included 612 Hindu widows who were less than one year of age, 2024 under ten years and 3,32,024 who were under fifteen years of age. The deplorable feature of the situation however is that the majority of these child widows were prevented by Hindu custom and usage from remarrying. L.S. Shastri writes: "Such a lamentable state of affairs exists in no country, civilized or uncivilized in the world. And it is high time that the law came to the assistance of these helpless victims of social customs. Whatever its origin or justification in old days, child marriage is admittedly out of date and source of untold misery and harm at present."[5]

In 1929 Child Marriage Restraint Act was passed, prohibiting child marriage below the age of 11 years for a Hindu girl and 15 years for a Hindu boy. However this act of 1929 was defective in many respects as the British subject under the British Empire was not made amenable to the above said act. So it was amended in 1938 and made applicable to everyone living in India. The bill is commonly known as Sharda Act of 1938. The age limit was revised and was set at 18 years for a Hindu boy and 14 years for a Hindu girl. This act was further revised in 1955. The age limit was fixed at 18 years for a boy and 16 years for a girl to contract a valid marriage, if they were not prohibited by other reservations mentioned in the Hindu Marriage Act, 1955.

In case a boy or a girl does not have his or her natural guardians but they or their property is under the superintendence of any court or any guardian, then the age limit is raised for a Hindu boy or a girl to 21 years and 18 years respectively. There is punishment prescribed for a male adult below 21 years of age marrying a child. If a male above 18 years of age and below 21 contracts child marriage, he is punishable with simple imprisonment which may extend to 15 days or with fines which may extend to Rs. 1000 or with both.

Dowry was one of the biggest social evils which was eating into the vitals of the Hindu society. Many parents had to toil all their lives and yet lead miserable lives because they had to arrange for dowry for the marriage of their daughters or sisters. Social reformers like Premchand raised their voice against this pernicious system. And later, legislation took up cudgels against it and placed on the statute book the Dowry Prohibition Act of 1961, with the professed object of putting a stop to the evil system of giving and taking dowry.

In this act, dowry means any property or valuable security given or agreed to be given either directly or indirectly, (a) by one party of a marriage to the other party of the marriage, (b) by the parents of either party of the marriage or any other person to either party of the marriage, or to any other person, as consideration for the marriage.

The bill however takes care to exclude presents in the form of clothes and ornaments etc. The limit of Rs. 2000 has been eliminated in the act as it has emerged from the legislative anvil. Therefore nuptials presents may be of any value howsoever high. Further, under this act, if any person, after the commencement of this act, demands directly or indirectly from the parents or guardians of a bride or bridegroom, as the case may be, any dowry, he is to be punished with imprisonment or fine, which may extend to Rs. 5000, or with both.[6] If any person, after the commencement of this act, gives or takes dowry, he is punishable with imprisonment which may extend to 6 months or with fine which may extend to Rs. 5000 or with both.

One more remarkable fact, which extends over the novels and short stories of Premchand, is his voice against corruption among government and high-levelled authorities. From a government servant of low wages to a high class senior officer could be easily silenced by the radiance of notes. This corruption was prevalent also among the police force. They accepted bribes; consequently the criminals were released and innocents were entangled in deceptive cases. The theme of Premchand's various novels as *Premashram* and *Gaban* revolves around such corruption. Premchand had a vivid dream to reform this evil.

One of the Indian Gazettes wrote: "The scope for bribery and corruption of public servants had been enormously increased by war conditions and though the war is now over, opportunities for corrupt practices will remain for a considerable time to come. Controls are being terminated, large amounts of government surplus stores are being disposed of; there will for years be shortage of various kinds requiring imposition of controls and extensive schemes of post-war reconstruction involving the disbursement of very large sums of government money. All these activities offer wide scope for corrupt practices. The seriousness of the evil and possibility of its continuance or extension in future are such as to justify immediate and drastic action to stamp it out. "[7]

And ultimately the prevention of corruption act (Act II of 1947) came to everyone's relief. According to this act: (1) A public servant is said to commit the offence of criminal misconduct (a) If he habitually accepts or obtains or agrees to accept or attempts to obtain from any person for himself or for any other person, any gratification as a motive or reward, or (b) If he habitually accepts or obtains or agrees to accept or attempts to obtain for himself or for any other person any valuable thing without consideration or for a consideration which he knows to be inadequate from any person, or (c) If he dishonestly or fraudulently misappropriates or otherwise converts for his own use any property entrusted to him or under his control as a public servant or allows any other person to do so, or (d) If he by corrupt or illegal means obtains for himself or any other person any valuable thing or pecuniary advantage or (e) If he or any person on his behalf is in possession or has, at any time during the period of his office been in possession, of pecuniary resources or property disproportionate to his known sources of income. (2) Any public servant who commits criminal misconduct shall be punishable with imprisonment for a term which shall not be less than one year but which may extend to seven years and shall also be liable to fine.

Further, there have been several amendments in this act so as to be applied more strictly. Moreover, to give proof of acceptance of bribes, new methods have been adopted. By the use of ultra-violet rays and anthracene powder, it can be detected that the accused had received the currency notes to which the powder had been applied. By the presence of powder on the hands or shirt of the accused, the prosecution may lead to positive evidence by way of expert evidence.

There is also phenolphthalein sodium carbonate test. This test is based on the fact that phenolphthalein is colourless in acid and neutral media and deep purple in alkaline. It is a coal tar produce and is available in the form of light powder. The currency notes or other articles intended for the purpose of bribe are coated with phenolphthalein powder. When a person touches these, his hands invariably collect a few particles of the powder. When these hands are dipped into a solution of sodium carbonate, the solution turns to purple or pink colour.

Although there is punitive legislation against taking bribes, it does not seem adequate because of other economic factors, which compel the alleged accused to be its prey. We hope that the evil featured in Premchand's novels most prominently will be removed as soon as possible, as a mark of tribute to the great writer.

Premchand unfolded scenes of rural poverty and its consequences in a number of his novels and short stories. In fact, his literary work is replete with the cries of a farmer, hard pressed under debt to the moneylenders. It may be Shankar of "Sava Seer Gahun" or Hori of *Godan* but the voice of Premchand is equally pained and critical. Throughout his life, he did his best to wipe out the tears from the eyes of such victims of feudal economy. The debtor had not only to repay the loan advanced to him by a moneylender but also had to work as a forced labour for the moneylender throughout his life. In many cases, even his children and grandchildren were made to work for the moneylender to repay the debts of his forefathers.

Illiteracy was rampant and added fuel to the fire in the game of moneylenders against farmers. Mahajans, landlords and moneylenders were exploiting and sapping the whole rural economy. A figure of Rs. 5 advanced to a farmer could be exploited to Rs. 500 or Rs. 5000 plus various interests charged by Mahajans on the principal amount were beyond the imagination of the poor farmer to liquidate them in his lifetime. Such a pitiable condition existed all around Premchand and it was the overall effect of such social reforms that government itself came to rescue the preys of Mahajans.

After India's freedom, democratic and welfare government emerged and the dreams of Premchand came true. Co-operative farming was encouraged and cooperative banks were set up in each village from where the needy farmers could take loans with easy terms to repay it with a much less rate of interest than a professional moneylender. Such facilities helped the farmers to stand on their feet. From time to time, various legislations were also passed to root-out this malady which crippled our rural society for centuries. The most drastic step in this regard was taken by the Central government in 1977 whereby the Union government, through a special ordinance, declared that all the loans and advances made by the Mahajans and moneylenders to poor farmers stand annulled. They were debarred from realising the money advanced by them. However, in some cases, the Government itself compensated them.

The poor farmers and tillers who were victims of moneylenders were also allowed to retain the piece of land which they had nourished with sweat and blood. Millions of poor people heaved a sigh of relief. The mission which Premchand had championed throughout his life had ultimately been achieved.

It is a common belief that the destiny of a nation is shaped in her classrooms. In a world based on science and technology, it is education that determines the level of prosperity, welfare and security of the people. On the equality and number of persons coming out of schools and colleges will depend our success in the great enterprise of national reconstruction, the principal objective of which is to raise the standard of living of our people.

In an agricultural country like India, more than 3/4th population is still illiterate. When Premchand wrote, there was a wide gulf between the rich and the poor. It was difficult for the poor to send their children to public schools where there was always a stress upon their dress and complexion instead of their mental make up. Hence, they usually took their primary education in schools called madrasa. Premchand himself received his primary education in such a madrasa. The teachers or maulavis of such schools hardly took any pain for the career of students.

The condition of girls was still worse. Due to the illiteracy of parents, the girls were mostly not allowed to cross the limits of their threshold. Those who received western education like Miss Malti of *Godan* were not honoured in the society of the times. It was alleged that they forgot their own culture and civilization in which they were brought up. Premchand boldly announced his deep dissatisfaction with these conditions.

After independence, our government has taken many progressive steps. In urban areas, education is provided both in English and Hindi medium. For children, there are primary schools. In many schools, there is a provision to teach gymnastic and swimming. All sorts of sports and physical exercises are taught regularly to the students.

For higher classes, there are numerous government high secondary schools and inter colleges. These have the facilities of good libraries, sports and science laboratories. Government grants are available for these schools and colleges. Merit scholarships are given to brilliant students and loan scholarships to the poor students.

The standard of postgraduate colleges is very high. The teachers of high calibre are appointed. Fee concessions are given to those who cannot afford the expenses of their study.

In villages, the picture is not as gloomy as it was earlier. Every villager and peasant has a feeling that his progeny should be educated. There is a provision for primary and high secondary schools. Fortunately, some states of India have announced and arranged free education upto tenth class.

Recently the government has taken remarkable steps for adult education. Trained teachers have been sent to teach those adults who nourish the desire of being educated. Night classes are held for those men and women who remain busy throughout